June, 2001

How much less Life is, because she's no longer alive, how much greater it is, because she was —

June 17, 2001, having planted a rose garden in her memory, enjoying some iced Tea and the sound of the breeze in the cottonwoods and spruces —

GOD'S DOG

CONVERSATIONS WITH COYOTE

WEBSTER KITCHELL

My thanks to Bob Stearns and others for encouraging me
to collect these adventures with Coyote.
Bob Stearns, Trish Judd, Don Bush, and Nancy Kitchell
all gave suggestions on the manuscript,
some of which I accepted, all of which I appreciate.
Bill Gannon was helpful with the publishing world.
Bonnie Bishop carried the project through professionally,
for which I am deeply grateful.
No one works alone, which is a great joy. W.K.

Copyright © 1991 by Webster Kitchell.
Published by Skinner House Books,
an imprint of the Unitarian Universalist Association,
25 Beacon Street, Boston, MA 02108-2800.
All rights reserved including the right to reproduce this book in any form.
Skinner House edition 1-55896-303-0
Library of Congress Catalog Card Number 91-65761
Book Design by Bonnie Bishop
Illustrations © Glen Strock
Typesetting by Buffalo Publications

Printed in the USA.

10 9 8 7 6 5
99 98 97

FOR THE
CONGREGATION
OF THE
UNITARIAN CHURCH OF SANTA FE,
MY FRIENDS
WHO ENCOURAGE THIS
DEEP FOOLISHNESS

CONTENTS

INTRODUCTION

Coyote came into my life unbidden, unwanted, un-yearned for. I had given up on God. I was living my life, and God was doing whatever God does. Perhaps I was understood by God, but I had accepted that I was never going to understand God.

Surprisingly this made no difference to my being a parish minister. Most of the people in the congregation had also given up trying to understand God. They would have been content to understand their children. So we worked together on such things; on understanding ourselves, our mates, our children, our society. We worked on that with an eye to becoming more human, more humane. That seems a good set of things for a little church to be doing. It might have been what God was wanting us to do all along.

So I was surprised to have Coyote enter my life. I met Coyote shortly before dawn on the summer solstice. There are coyotes, and there is Coyote. I met a coyote that morning in the desert, but before the day was over, I met Coyote, the Trickster. That's what happens when Coyote is around.

It was at Ghost Ranch, near Santa Fe, New Mexico, I was to meet some people and hike to Chimney Rock to greet the sun on the solstice. I overslept, as is my custom. Hurrying along a trail in the pre-dawn light, I caught a coyote out of the corner of my eye. She or he was on a cross-trail to mine. We saw each other at the same time. We stopped and looked into each other's eyes. It seemed to me we held the gaze for a long time. Then the coyote trotted across my path, headed home after a night on the mesa. I went up the trail to the sunrise.

All day that summer solstice day the coyote's gaze was in my awareness.

Our group met for a sundown ceremony. The drums and the words were in the Native American tradition. After 45 minutes of drumming, chanting, and meditating, the shaman asked us to close our eyes for a vision-quest. I closed my eyes. I had a vision of a naked male child with blond curls standing before imposing closed doors, doors reminscent of a Spanish colonial church. Startled, I opened my eyes. Everyone had their eyes closed. I closed mine, and the vision was still there. The vision was accompanied by a great sense of peace, of well-being.

The ceremony over, I tempted the shaman with some beers to come sit by the campfire. I brought up the subject of the vision and meeting the coyote. As we discussed it, I came to the startling possibility that I might be ready for a spiritual renewal, and that Coyote might be my spirit-guide. My left-brain was shocked. But my right-brain was enthusiastic.

Being an intellectual philosopher therapist sort of minister, I read up on Coyote. Not on coyotes, which have limited appeal, but on Coyote the Trickster, a semi-divine character in the mythology of all the Native American people. When Coyote is around, there's going to be trouble, and often trouble of a ridiculous sort. More often than not the tricks of the Trickster backfire on the Trickster himself. As I intellectually boned up on the Trickster, my unconscious kept interrupting to say; "This is the story of your life!"

So it has been. I have never outsmarted anyone more than I have outsmarted myself. Every best intention has turned into an exploding cigar. I identified with Wile E. Coyote questing for the Holy Grail, played in the cartoons by the Roadrunner.

Then one day Coyote himself walked into my study as I was about to write a sermon.

COYOTE LOOKS AT PROGRESS
AND WONDERS IF IT IS

Leaning back in my chair, I tried to summon an opening for a sermon on Progress. A rustle distracted me. I looked over to my green leather sofa and saw Coyote materialize. He looked elegant. He was wearing a mink coat and an Aussie hat.

"Wow!" I said. "I hoped you'd show up, but I didn't really expect it. I mean being reasonable and liberal and educated, such things aren't supposed to happen to me."

"Think of it as a dispensation from the gods," he said, smiling benignly. "You opened yourself up to the spirit of enchantment out there in the desert. You accepted the vision that rose out of yourself. You did not reject the possibility of magic in your life. So here I am. But if I bother you, I can leave."

"No," I said, "Don't leave. I've been playing it too safe. I want to know what the Trickster has to say."

He smiled a conspiratorial smile. "You haven't exactly played it safe! That's why you have been given this dispensation! The gods like your spirit and want to encourage it!"

I was mightily pleased. We grinned at each other. What a reward after 30 years in the ministry! Progress!

I said, "You look so elegant! Do you dress this way all the time?"

"No, no! Only in Santa Fe. In Santa Fe I am a celebrity. I have to do my part on the conspicuous consumption front."

"How do you dress other places?"

"In my old coyote fur. But in Santa Fe where I get a commission on all the wooden coyotes the galleries sell, I am a celebrity. I have my public and my image to consider."

With just a little sarcasm I asked, "Do you eat at the Coyote Cafe?"

"Only if there is roadrunner on the menu."

"I'm glad you're here," I said. "I need some help on a sermon about Progress. It looks as though you have made progress coming in off the range to make a killing off the tourists."

I had caught his interest and his vanity.

He lit a Santa Fe brand cigarette. "Natural," he said, "no unhealthy additives!" He pulled a cold L.A. Beer out of his pocket, thought a moment, grinned, and said, "Yeah, I guess you could call this progress!"

"I was reading something by Richard Feynman, the Nobel Prize winning physicist, and he said words to the effect that if you took everything the ancients knew and everything we modern humans know and put them all together, you'd have to admit that we don't know anything . . . about the meaning, I mean."

"So what's that got to do with Progress?" he asked.

"Well, I would think that if humanity had made any progress the past few millenia, we might have made some progress in understanding how to create a kinder, gentler civilization. I would think that with all the philosophers and theologians putting all that energy into wondering about the meaning of things, we would have come up with some idea of what it all means; what this pain and joy and love and hate and war and technology all mean; what they're for."

"Nah," said Coyote, "Progress means you get to drive faster in cooler-looking cars."

"Hey, that just means more coyotes get to be road kills."

He blanched, but he didn't say anything. He took off his hat and mink coat and threw them on the floor and lay back in his old coyote fur and scratched himself vigorously and happily and obscenely.

"You may be on to something. Maybe it looks like Progress, but really it's the same old disasters in new forms."

"My congregation isn't going to like that," I said. "We have been preaching the progress of mankind onward and upward forever. We have been assuring ourselves that humanity can pull itself up by its own bootstraps if humanity really wants to. We are convinced that we are the ones called by our own Ultimate Goodness to convince humanity of that. If we could just get humanity to listen to us and be reasonable."

Coyote leered.

"Now come on, Coyote, there's lots of people who hope that the leaders of the US and USSR are going to bring peace and international harmony to the world. The Cold War is over, China and the Soviet Union are rediscovering freedom, and we're going to have free trade and computer links everywhere. Military spending will be diverted to low-cost geodesic domes for peasants everywhere. Maybe the Jews and the Palestinians will even come to respect each other."

"If I thought you people really believed that," said Coyote, "I'd hang around some other church. That's whistling Dixie while Wall Street burns! You have to stop looking at the Big Picture if you want to believe in Progress. Just look at the little picture. Then you can see progress. You've got a free society, right? That means a guy can start out poor and with luck and a little larceny, he can end up rich. That's progress. In Europe in the fifteenth century a person couldn't do that. In the Asian part of the Soviet Union 70 years ago people didn't have decent water, and there was a conquest every other Thursday. Now they have decent water and can commit Socialist larceny and take life easy. That's progress! Feynman is right; looking at the big picture, it's hard to say any more than that the big wheel goes round, and then it goes round again. But if you concentrate on the small picture such as the development of the answering machine or ski technology, then there's real progress.

"You're a total cynic, Coyote!"

"Sure I am, and so are you. You are either a fool or a cynic if you think you can convince people there is Progress in the Big Picture. You may have a few naive folks in your congregation, but I'll bet most of them are card-carrying cynics."

"So why do they hang around a nineteenth century church with a doctrine of Progress?"

"Being a cynic doesn't mean you have to be a *cynic*," he said. "It is one thing to be an intellectual cynic and understand that we really know nothing when it comes to the Big Picture. It is another thing to be mean about it. There are cynics whose cynicism leads them to be mean and angry, and there are cynics whose cynicism leads them to humility. Now that's progress when cynicism leads to humility."

"You're confusing me."

"No, I'm not. It's just that you don't want to act on what you know is true. Anyone who knows there is no progress in the long run has made personal progress in the short run. That person has been disillusioned, and getting disillusioned is always progress because illusions, no matter how rosy and pleasant, are always a fog between one's perception and what is real. When you travel 75 miles an hour down the freeway in a heavy fog, you're making fast progress toward real disaster."

Coyote had turned very serious. We looked at each other a moment. Then I said, "So disillusionment and cynicism are the first steps in an individual's progress toward being real?"

"Right! You knew that! Paul Tillich taught you that 35 years ago."

"You know about Paul Tillich?"

"Hey, I was there! Tillich and I worked together for years. That's why you liked what he said. His coyote spoke to your coyote. That man liked it out on the edge."

"So this leads us to the edge?"

"Hey, that's the only place you *can* live. I don't mean going fast in a plastic car; that *is* driving on the edge, but it's not what I mean. I mean moving through cynicism and disillusionment to affirming life and love anyway despite everything. Despite not knowing the Big Picture. Despite knowing it's all going to crash into the big brick wall at the end of the universe. Despite all that, if you choose to live with love and compassion and laughter, man, that's progress!"

"But, Coyote, wasn't it progress when people came here from Europe, and then the people in the east came west, and eventually we have places like Albuquerque and Phoenix and Los Angeles?"

"Partly true, but you have to remember why they left where they were. They left where they were because it was too civilized. The ordinary peo-ple said, 'Dear God, civilization is a bore!' They thought it couldn't be any worse out west with the blizzards and droughts and hostile Apaches. Now that was progress for those people. Of course it wasn't progress for the Apaches or coyotes."

"So you think it's the rebels and mischief-makers who make progress?"

"Right!" Coyote grinned. "Without the mischief-makers there isn't any progress. There's just the dull inhumane boring status-quo mean judgemental culture; just Victorian piety!"

"Let me get this straight. You think I should tell this nice liberal intell-igent congregation that the only progress there is has its basis in cynicism, disillusion, rebelliousness and mischief-making?"

"You got it, baby!" and he stood up and started putting on his coat.

"They're not going to like it."

"Trust me! They're all coyotes in disguise."

"Maybe I should say Tillich told me this."

"Suit yourself, but I'm more fashionable than Tillich. When a person gets past the illusions, she or he becomes healthily cynical about the politicians and historians who try to portray us as better than we really are. When people come to understand how little we know, and accept that being civilized is a bore, well then they can live on the edge and forgive other people for not being any better than humans are. And that, my friend, is progress!"

I couldn't resist a little dig after he had disposed of my good rhetoric. "So, how come you're wearing a mink coat? Don't you have any respect for your fellow fur-bearing creatures?"

He grinned condescendingly.

"All road kills, baby. This one by a Mercedes. This one by a Camry. This one by a truck full of illegals coming up from El Paso. Here, you can have it!"

He disappeared, and I have this great mink coat that fits perfectly. I guess that's progress.

Don Coyote Meets Don Quixote

he congregation was delighted by Coyote's views on progress. I enjoyed the compliments, but I was not at all sure I could contact him when I needed him. I decided to sneak off to the donut shop and think about it. There was Coyote at the counter. He flicked his tail in recognition, and I sat next to him.

"So, what's happening?" he asked.

"Nothing. How's by you?"

"Bored. Nothing happening in town and nothing happening out of town."

"We could do a little cruising," I said. "I need to talk to you."

"Saturday afternoon and you don't have your sermon ready?"

"You got it!" We got a dozen suger-bombs at the counter, put the top down on my Mexican Volkswagen, and rode off into a gathering snowstorm.

"So, what's this sermon about?" He pulled his fur coat up around his ears and popped a lemon-filled donut into his mouth.

"It's about a fellow who lived in a small town and got so bored and crazy reading about the knights of old he finally went in search of romance and adventure."

"I can identify with him," he said.

"So can most red-blooded males and at least half the red-blooded females."

"Who was this fellow?"

"Don Quixote."

"*Donald* Coyote? Never met him."

"Not Donald! Don! And not Coyote. Quixote!"

"Why do you call him 'Don' if his name isn't 'Donald'?"

"It's a spanish term of respect, Coyote."

"Ah, that explains all the street signs in Santa Fe. Don Diego. Don Gaspar. I always thought it was peculiar so many of these Spanish fellows had the same first name. A title of respect? Could I be Don Coyote?"

"I suppose, but I think you will have to clean up your act if you want to be known as Don Coyote."

"So tell me about Don Quixote and maybe I'll learn to be respectable and have some adventures, too. I am sorely lacking in both."

"If you want respect, you shouldn't be riding in this old yellow VW Thing. You need to get a suit and a necktie and a Volvo."

"So I'll skip the respectability and settle for the adventure. What did Don Quixote do that was adventurous?"

"Nothing really. It was in his head. His most famous adventure was when he was all dressed up as a knight looking for someone to rescue, but it seemed it was just a dull summer day in rural Spain. Then he saw a field of windmills with their sails going round, and he thought it was a field of giants. He attacked!"

"God," said Coyote, "Didn't anyone tell him they were just windmills?"

"His squire tried to tell him, but Don Quixote told him to pray. He shouted at the windmills, 'Fly not, cowards!' A breeze began to blow and the windmills began to turn. Don Quixote commended himself to his Lady Dulcinea and charged. The blade of the windmill caught his lance and tumbled the Don and his horse over and over. Sancho Panza, his squire, picked him up and said, 'I told you they were windmills.' But Don Quixote said, 'You don't understand, Sancho Panza, a cruel magician changed the giants into windmills.' "

"This poor old Don is nuts."

"Of course, but that's what happens when people get bored hanging around a small town with nothing to do. They start making things up and talking about the neighbors just to get something going."

Coyote looked at me. "You wouldn't be talking about Don Coyote, would you?"

"I'm talking about everyone. Everyone has some craziness and some need for adventure. Everyone finds being respectable mind-splittingly dull at times. That's why we watch violence on TV and drive too fast and eat things loaded with cholesterol. That's why people are glad to see you coming, Old Trickster."

"Yeah—you know what gets me? What gets me is in the summertime all these nice people from Dallas and Los Angeles come to Santa Fe looking for a little adventure. They go out after supper and stroll around the Plaza and have an ice cream cone. Then they stroll around the Plaza again and have another ice cream cone. Then the awful truth dawns on them. They have just done it all, twice, and it's only 8:30. They have bought the kids new outfits and driven all that distance, and that's it! The locals have all gone home to watch violence on TV."

"You got it, Coyote! Poor old Don Quixote began to believe all those books he'd read about romance and adventure."

Coyote looked unnerved. "Didn't anyone *do* anything?"

"While he was recovering they plastered up the door to the room where he had all the romantic books. After he got well and started looking for the room, everyone said, 'What roomful of books?'"

"Did he give up and forget about it?"

"No, because he had a dream. He was living in a romantic world that was so much more fun than his ordinary life in a little Spanish town. He thought he was a great knight and loved a beautiful lady. He was full of honor and purity and goodness and morality and courage."

"Are you telling me that all that good stuff Don Quixote believed in is madness and that reality is being stuck in a small town with nothing to do and no way out? You sound like a Communist existentialist!" He glared at me.

"My opinion, Coyote, is that there are good days and bad days."

"Which is this?"

"This is the best," I said diplomatically. "What could be better than cruising in an old jalopy with someone whose fur coat covers his whole face? Have you seen any girls waving to us?"

"*You* invited *me*!" he said, looking straight ahead.

"Don Coyote, don't be offended. I respect you. I am saying I enjoy your company even when nothing is happening. There is nothing better than hanging around with your friends, Don Coyote. That's why streets have corners; so people can hang around on them. But most people are so busy walking down the sidewalk to get somewhere, they never hang around on the corner and just watch."

"I am glad to see you are learning something from hanging out with me."

"On, no, Don Coyote. I learned *that* when I was 13 and hung out at the general store on the town common. My poor mother was sure I was learning bad things, which I was, eagerly. But there wasn't anyone else to hang around with, so what could she do, poor lady?"

"I am glad you realize now how she suffered. Such a noble woman. Say, what was Don Quixote's relationship with the Lady Dulcinea?"

"Pure romance. Entirely without lechery. He really didn't need her. All he needed was his image of her to keep him fired up with romance and fantasy. Cervantes, the author of the story, has Don Quixote describe her this way:

> "She is my queen and mistress; her beauty superhuman; her hair is gold, her forehead the Elysian fields, her eyebrows rainbows, her eyes suns, her cheeks roses, her lips coral, pearls her teeth, alabaster her neck, marble her bosom, ivory her hands, and her complexion snow, and those parts which modesty has veiled from human sight are such, I think and trust, that discretion can praise them, but make no comparison.' "

Don Coyote looked at me with shock. "Her bosom is marble?" He thought about that. "Marble is a cold stone, right?"

I nodded.

He said softly, "She's got a cold stone bosom? He's a madman, sure enough."

I nodded.

"Did I ever tell you about the cold night I seduced the maiden?"

"I read about it in the Navajo stories. The relationship between Don Quixote and the Lady Dulcinea was nothing like that!"

"Why would anyone want to have any other sort of relationship than I had with that maiden? I don't understand you humans. You live so much in your dreams, in your fantasies, in your misperceptions of reality. You're all like Don Quixote. Your fantasy life is everything; those parts of the body which modesty has veiled from human sight, as Don Quixote so delicately put it. Notice that he wasn't above thinking of such things; he was just above admitting that he thought of such things. So he went around the country making a fool of himself while he could have been enjoying himself and making his Lady Dulcinea happy too. You human beings are so confused!"

I was feeling defensive. "You're the one who said you were bored."

"But that was reality. I knew I was bored, but I also knew if I hung around for awhile someone interesting would come along, and here we are cruising along having fun discussing this romantic jerk friend of yours. Most humans seem to think happiness is somewhere over the rainbow, and if life isn't gracious and good and beautiful and sweet, someone must be to blame. Or they go on a guilt trip and blame *themselves* for life not being beautiful all the time. It really gets me angry at you creatures! You try to make Santa Fe not true to life, but true to the travel fantasy magazines. So people come rushing over here to realize their fantasy and end up wondering where the action is. They want life to be provided for them, and they want life to be perfect! They are contemporary Don Quixotes looking for some perfect stone-cold bosom to give them life."

I was quiet. He had slumped in the seat, nursing his anger. Suddenly he said.

"Let me out. Stop here!"

"We're way out in the desert, Coyote."

"I know. Thanks for the ride. I'm sick of being in town listening to you humans."

And with that he loped easily across the desert and was gone. I thought about following him, but it was snowy and getting dark and I had a sermon to write. I put the top up, put in the side curtains, turned on the heat, and headed for Santa Fe.

Coyote Says He Never Lies

beautiful day in New Mexico. I was out by La Bajada, where Interstate 25 climbs up to Santa Fe. The view there is majestic. I saw a dirt track going to the edge of the escarpment, so I put the top down, and very soon Coyote ran alongside and jumped in the back seat.

"I can't resist this yellow car with the top down. You know how to get to me!"

"Why don't you sit up front?"

"I like it in back. Makes me feel like a Governor. Where's the crowd? Where's the ticker-tape?"

"I came out here to get away from town, Coyote. Someday, though, we'll get the City Council to proclaim Coyote Day. I'll drive you up San Francisco Street. We'll get the congregation out there waving banners and cheering."

"I'd like that! Would you really do that for me?"

"Absolutely!"

"You're lying, but I appreciate the fantasy. Would there be drum majorettes in skimpy costumes?"

"Seems appropriate for Coyote Day."

"You're lying, but I love it."

"Don't you ever lie?"

"Never!" he roared, "I am a semi-divinity! I have certain standards to live up to. I would never lie!"

"You're lying!"

He laughed. "That's what I like about our relationship. We never lie to each other. We are always straightforward and honest with each other, right?"

"I know I am, but I'm not sure about you."

"Well said! And you never will be sure. Which makes it interesting. Let us agree that we will always be honest with each other, but we will never be sure of that. So we will always be suspicious of each other, too."

"That sounds like an honest relationship. I'll take it!"

"So, why are you out in the desert away from your own kind? Those human lies get too much for you?"

"Something like that. I think there is a federal law against honesty and plain speech in Washington. Then there's the New Mexico legislature."

"I feel as a Trickster I am getting some competition from the legislators."

We reached the edge of La Bajada, got out, and stood on the edge of the great lava flow overlooking the Rio Grande rift and the remains of a great volcano, now the Jemez range. The sun was bright, the wind was soft, and the traffic on the Interstate was miniature, a little ribbon of civilization in hundreds of square miles of desert, mountain, and sky.

"Nothing personal," said Coyote, "but I really don't like your kind. I think First Woman made a mistake when she created you as a specie. You humans are coming to be a real curse on the planet. Nothing personal. Some of you I like individually. I find you entertaining in a Coyote sort of way. But by and large you live in a weird world in your heads. You live in a complicated set of lies, both personal and social, which you believe even when they obviously don't work. I think you humans are a threat to us all."

I didn't have an answer to that. It is hard to hear your whole specie denigrated by a semi-divine presence. Still, he had said it wasn't personal, so I tried not to be defensive, to keep it high and theoretical. Which in my mind was a lie. It is hard to look at what humans have done, are doing, and probably will continue to do. I would have preferred to be Coyote and be able to view humanity as dispensable.

"Look at that lava flow," he said. "I don't know how old it is as you humans measure time. There really isn't such a thing as time for Coyotes. But think how long it's been there, slowing crumbling over the softer material underneath it. Think how unbelieveably long ago that soft under material was created. Think that all that is minor compared to what is happening to the earth's surface at this Rio Grande rift. Think that the Rio Grande rift is a minor thing in the slow plastic motion of the earth's crust. Think about that as a reality that is *not* going on in your mind. Just stand here and let it seep into your awareness."

So I stood there and let it seep into my awareness.

"How do you know all this about the earth's history?"

"You forget I am a semi-divine being. Actually, I took a course at the Community College."

I had no idea which was the truth, but it was encouraging to think that semi-divine presences were taking courses at the Community College.

"Coyote, what you say is true. And it's also true that humans as a specie are probably more of a curse on the planet than a blessing. That's true, Coyote. But, Coyote, but . . . BUT!"

"But what?"

"But there's *today*, Coyote! Don't you see, Coyote? There's *today*! There's this sunlight shining on us standing in a desert place looking at all this beauty, talking about something that moves me to tears. *That's* but what! *Joy*, Coyote!"

"Yes," he said, not smiling. "Yes, I see. There is this moment, and there wouldn't be this moment if there weren't you and me as individuals in this life standing here caring about it and wondering about it and enjoying it. You're right, there is this moment."

"There's a wise human being, in the best sense of being wise, named Joseph Campbell. He said there are times when the eternal enters the moment of time and space."

Coyote was thoughtful. "So you're saying that this moment when we feel alive and comprehend a little bit of the whole that underlies this moment and made it possible—the whole star story and planet story and life evolution story—this moment is a moment when eternity enters time and space and particularity?"

"Yes," I said. I didn't dare say more.

"Well," he said solemnly, "maybe there is some reason you humans evolved. I've never got a satisfactory answer when I howled in the night asking the divine bureacracy why you're here."

"I'm sure it's what justifies our existence. But perhaps that is a human hangup; having to justify our existence."

"No, everything has to justify its existence or its ceases to exist. I am a scavenger. I sing songs in the night. I do what I am supposed to do. Every specie has an obligation to the whole. You humans have forgotten that. You think your only obligation is to yourself."

"That's our lie. That we think we are special."

"That's your lie," he agreed.

I was wound up. I went on. "I think the lies we tell are so deep and so ingrained in our minds through our society and our history, through our needfulness and greed and will to power, that we have become so crazy we think sanity is nuts. There is such a disparity between the truth and what we say is true, that we either have to turn away and live private lives or embrace the lies and defend the lies as our public spokesmen do on TV night after night. That is why we bow down to people who systematically cheat us and exploit us. That is why we are powerless against the garbage that will bury us and all the desert. The garbage no one wants in their backyard and the garbage of a society that won't pay nurses or teachers a living wage or even treat them with respect . . ."

I turned and yelled at the miniature traffic below us on the Interstate, "Garbage! Garbage! Garbage!"

Coyote looked at the traffic. "No one seems to be stopping. Feeling a little desperate?"

"I feel desperate when I am in the places of humanity and hear all the lies about the glory of our wars; about how we have to keep the Cold War alive so there will be employment in New Mexico. Our federal officials ask us to have confidence in their treatment of nuclear waste even as they cover up the incompetence of the past 30 years. It would be one thing if they said they had made mistakes, but the record shows they lied even to themselves. Now it will be good for poor old New Mexico to take the nuclear garbage. It will create jobs; the pay-off!"

"Which lies am I to believe, Coyote? I suppose I want to believe some of the lies, because if I don't believe any of the lies, I will have to agree with you that humanity is a very bad design, even from our own human point of view. It's crazy-making to hear the lies repeated and repeated and repeated with pompous political gravity. Whether it's nuclear waste or political speeches, it's all garbage!"

"So, give me the car keys and jump off the cliff," Coyote jeered.

"It's too nice a day! Who would willingly leave such a beautiful world?"

"Is it just the beautiful day that keeps you here?" he asked quietly.

"That's a lot of it, but not the whole thing."

"Is there anything redeeming in the place where humans congregate? I can see this lonely beauty refreshes you, but is there anything back there where the people are that attracts you?"

I thought to myself, this Coyote is a good counselor. I'm glad I found him. I wonder if I could tell the congregation I had found a god who was willing to listen sympathetically.

"Yes, Coyote, there is. There are a few poets who speak the truth. They write small volumes that don't sell. Most poets are never known because we reward only the big liars. It's hard to write poetry that tells lies because a poem has to have the same sort of integrity that this expanse of desert has. A poem has to have a hard burning bit of truth in it to move people."

"I've never had experience with poetry. I'll settle for the moon and the stars and open country and some coyotes to swap stories with."

"In church the other day I read the congregation a sonnet by Bill Shakespeare. It was about truth in love. Shakespeare says one of the pleasures of love is the lies that lovers tell each other; and believe, even though they know better. As Bill says, 'And so I lie with her and she with me, and in our faults by lies we flattered be.' In his view, the lies of love make life bearable and thus become a sort of sublime honesty, which is that we cannot live without love and would lie to get it."

"Why don't you humans just be truthful! *I* never lie!"

"Then how come there are those stories of you lying?"

"Lies, all of them!" But he looked embarrassed. "I am semi-divine; therefore people tell stories about me. Humans project their own nature onto me. They assume that because they lie, I lie. But the real me is animal nature, and animal nature never lies. The trouble with you humans is that weird mind. Somewhere along the evolutionary line you left your animal nature behind. You left behind its truth. You even tell lies about your animal nature, calling it bad or "lower." Your stuff about spirituality and nobility is mostly lies you tell yourself. I wish I could see you humans celebrate your animal nature and understand you don't live apart from nature. If you really have a wondrous generous noble spiritual nature, I wish you'd let the rest of us see it occasionally. Your noble lies blind you to your meanness and selfishness and cruelty."

"I have noticed," he went on, "that humans are the easiest specie to con. I don't know a rabbit or a chipmunk who would take the guff you take from each other. When I come around the other animals, they say, 'Scram, Coyote, old Trickster. Get lost!' When I hang around humans, they like as not elect me Governor. I have been Governor of a lot of states, which may explain why I like riding in the backseat with the top down." He glared at me.

Changing the subject, I said, "Getting back to Shakespeare, Bill said in another sonnet that he was once unkind to his love. He is glad he was, for now she has been unkind to him, and he can understand how she felt. So her unkindness ransoms him, and his unkindness ransoms her".

"You weird humans, I don't get it," scoffed Coyote.

"I suppose it is weird to a divinity. What it means is that if we can get out of our lies and understand that the best of us cause pain, and that much of the pain that has been inflicted on us was not meant as anything personal, then perhaps we can forgive each other and ourselves for what we've done. If we can liberate ourselves from the lies and weirdness of our society and our minds, we can live with some dignity and grace. We can live in that real love that accepts us as we are, without any need for lies."

He gazed at me for a long time.

"You think you can go back to that place where humans congregate and live in all that garbage you were talking about and experience dignity and grace and love and honesty? You really think you can do that?"

He was incredulous.

"I *know* I can. What's more, most humans seem to be able to do it a good bit of the time. It's really what being human is about."

"I'll be damned. Maybe I won't give up on you yet."

We looked at the miniature cars on the Interstate hurrying between Albuquerque and Santa Fe.

Coyote said, "You sit in back and pretend you're the Governor. I'll drive!"

So we came back, and I think the jackrabbits are still talking about the yellow Volkswagen Thing with Coyote driving and some guy waving to them from the backseat.

COYOTE MEETS JESUS

 uddenly a dust-devil mixed with a burst of rain swept through the car. I wiped my eyes and was greeted by Coyote in the seat next to me.

"I must get a car with roll-up windows," I said.

"Then you wouldn't have any mythical desert characters blowing into your life!" He smirked.

"Do you know Jesus?" he asked.

"Coyote, don't tell me you've become a born again Christian!"

"I've been born again many a time, but never as a Christian. I was hanging around the library trying to pick up chicks, and this chick asked me if I knew Jesus. She pronounced it 'Geezus,' not 'Hey-soos,' but I knew who she meant. I said I didn't know him, and she said maybe I should try hanging around a church and get to know Jesus instead of hanging around the library being a wolf. Imagine! She didn't know the difference between a coyote and a wolf. I thought I would check with the only minister I know and see if he can introduce me to Jesus."

"Glad to!" I said.

We stopped at the donut shop, and I got him a dozen sugar-glazed and an oat-bran muffin for myself.

"What's with the oat-bran?"

"I'm not one of the immortals."

"Tough!" And he scarfed down two disgusting beautiful chocolate-covered sugar-bombs.

"I may get a car with automatic electric Coyote locks!" I said, resentfully.

"Knock it off! You need me!"

We went to my office. I opened the Gospel of Matthew, and Jesus stepped out. I introduced them.

Coyote said, "I really liked that movie about you where you got down off the cross and got married and had some children and then went back up on the cross A very clever trick! I liked that."

"Thank you," said Jesus. "That's my favorite of the movies they've done of my life. I enjoy your movies, too."

Coyote seemed shy. "You mean the Roadrunner cartoons?"

"Yes," said Jesus. "They're favorites in heaven."

I said, "I had no idea they watched old cartoons in heaven. Wait til the congregation hears *that*!"

Jesus shrugged. "There's a lot of time to kill in eternity."

Suddenly I was glad not to be one of the immortals, but I kept my opinion to myself.

Coyote offered Jesus the last donut.

Jesus said, "Oh, I couldn't take the last one."

"Oh, go ahead. The reverend says they're bad for me."

"Let's have another round," said Jesus. Suddenly the one donut became a dozen donuts with some fish-sticks mixed in.

So they lit into the fish-sticks and donuts while I made tea. I assure you that the conversation I have recorded is gospel.

Coyote started off. "There are a few things about your system, Jesus, that I want to ask about. I admire what you did. I liked your raising the dead. Palm Sunday in the temple was great theater. I liked the way you handled the temptations out in the desert. I agree that people and divine beings like us do not live by bread alone. Life is a lot more than getting fed. I like the idea that you shouldn't test your god. Gods can't be trusted any more than humans can not to give in to the Trickster impulse. So when the devil said 'Jump!', you were right not to do it. Very sound! Very sound! Don't tempt God!"

Jesus looked pleased and licked the frosting off a donut.

"And I liked the part about resisting the temptation to use your powers to have dominion over the world. Humans don't seem to understand that — though the reverend here doesn't even have windows in his car, so maybe he's an exception."

I kept quiet, but silently I objected that my car does have side curtains. It's just a bother to stop and put them on.

"Yes," said Jesus, "I notice he doesn't even have a computer in his office. Which maybe is why I like him in spite of his regrettable Unitarian theology."

Coyote went on. "What I don't understand is your emphasis on humans being perfect even as God is perfect. You must know humans don't have it in them to be perfect. If they try being perfect, it spoils them as humans."

"Ultimately, you're right," said Jesus. "You have to understand what we were trying to do. These were the early days of civilization, and humans were fascinated by all the new rules thay had made up so their civilization would work. They were trying to live their lives by rules; do this, do that. They thought if they did the rules just right, everything would be OK. I was sent by the heavenly forces to get them to loosen up a little. Have a party with the publicans and tax collectors. Leave the poor adulterers alone . . . they've got enough trouble without being stoned. If your son comes home with a hangover, don't ask where he's been. Make him a good breakfast and some strong coffee."

"Ah, you are a being after my own heart," said Coyote, and went on to ask,

"What about this turning the other cheek when someone smites you? What about this advice that if someone asks for your coat, give him your coat and your shirt, too?"

"Again," said Jesus, "You have to remember the times. This was the beginning of humans amassing wealth. Greed makes humans less human, but greed was being promoted. People like Pontius Pilate were saying there is no such thing as truth. Which is untrue! You agree?"

"Oh, yes," said Coyote, "But the reverend here has been trying to convert me to logical positivism and relativism and other unsound secular doctrines."

Jesus looked at me disapprovingly. Coyote smirked. I gave my best, "Who, me?" shrug.

"Which truth were you referring to as untrue?" asked Coyote.

Jesus gave him a glance, sighed, and said sadly, "The truth I think I am talking about is the same one I was talking with Satan about — the truth that humans lose their humanity when they get greedy. They lose their humanity when they lust for power. They lose their humanity when they take their religion too seriously and tempt God. They lose their humanity when they think thay can live life by the rule-book. They lose their humanity when they think women and men live by bread alone."

"Right," said Coyote. "Same truth I believe in."

"Me, too," I thought.

Jesus said to Coyote, "You know the story I like best about you? The one of your seducing the maiden who said she'd marry you if you came back to life three times. But after she killed you three times, and you'd come back to life three times, she still wouldn't marry you. So you pretended to be cold and asked for a corner of her blanket. Pretty soon you were under the blanket and she was under you. From what the Navajos say, you both greatly enjoyed the night. Now that's life, I say!"

"Yes," chuckled Coyote, "that was a high point. Which was why I was so glad to see you give in to the last temptation."

Seeing my chance, I asked Jesus a question I'd always wanted to ask. "What did you mean when you said that anyone who would follow you must give up himself . . . or herself?"

"Those words were misunderstood and misused by the Church. I meant it in the Buddhist sense of giving up self. I learned it direct from the Buddha himself. But the Church used my words to control people politically, make them do what the Church wanted them to do. I shouldn't have said it. It was misunderstood and misused."

I suddenly felt much closer to Jesus. We smiled at each other.

Coyote got back in. "You know, I liked your parable of the workers in the field. I like the idea that those who come in at the last hour get just as much in wages as those who have worked all day. That's a good one! Enlightenment is like that; it's not something that comes to everyone at the same stage of life. Some attain enlightenment early, and some gain it at the last minute. But it's all the same; it's all enlightenment. It isn't something you earn. It's more like grace. It's given by God. People don't achieve it; they simply receive it if they open up to it."

"Yes," said Jesus, "it's like the Navajo chant about walking in beauty. Anyone can walk in beauty if they will see the beauty because the beauty is all around us. Before us, behind us, above us, below us, all around us is beauty, and anyone can walk in it. It isn't earned, so it doesn't matter how long you worked in the field; all day or an hour."

"It seemed unfair, though, to the people who had worked in the field all day," said Coyote.

Jesus nodded. "But they had strayed from the primitive knowledge that the lilies of the field toil not. They were into the early-capitalist go-by-the-book civilized rules. Under all the civilization and capitalist glory and power trips and intellectual arrogance, grace is still grace. It's a free gift from God. Like beauty. Those who get it earlier simply have the blessing of living with grace longer than those who get it late in life. Pity, if you must pity, those who never drop their civilized ways and never open up to grace."

"Another question," I said. "Why did you tell people to do their religion in private? Why did you tell them to go into a closet to pray? I like religion that is done in communities. This congregation sings and laughs together, and they share their lives. That seems better than going into a closet to pray."

"I agree," said Jesus. "I just meant that occasionally it's good to get off by yourself and think about what's important without all the distractions. I like to see a little introspection. Its good for humans.

"And the resurrection," I continued, "What about the resurrection?"

"Well, what about it?" asked Coyote. "We do that sort of thing all the time."

"Right," said Jesus. "That's nothing special for a divinity."

"Right," I said, but there was tone of resentment.

"Oh, come on, Reverend!" said Coyote. "We all know you've pulled off a few personal resurrections of your own. You've been recycled."

I was delighted to have such wonderful friends. We laughed and finished off the donuts.

"I've got an idea!" said Coyote. "Let's all ride down to Cochiti Lake in the Reverend's old Volkswagen, and, Jesus, you can teach us the walking-on-water trick."

So that's what we did. Coyote learned it very quickly, but I got terribly wet and never got the hang of it. Coyote made a fire and Jesus made some wine and I taught them some old union songs, and we had a wonderful time.

COYOTE DOESN'T WANT TO KNOW
WHY THE UNIVERSE

hrough the crack in my study door came a hairy snout followed by two yellow eyes followed by two large ears.

"What you doing, man?"

"Reading a book, Coyote. *A Brief History of Time* by Stephen Hawking*."

"Why would you read something like that?"

"Well, it's philosophical. I do philosophy. He wonders about why we're here and It's here."

"Why would he wonder about that?"

"Some humans wonder about those things. Stephen Hawking says the Universe is finite, but without boundaries."

He studied his nails, "That's news?"

"It is to a lot of people. It was news to me."

"You humans!" he burst out. "You are so smart you take all the fun out of life. The animals know the Universe is finite, but without boundaries! You humans don't seem to know anything until some mathematician says its true, and even then you're just believing what he tells you. You aren't experiencing for yourself what it means to say the Universe is boundless but finite. *Life* is boundless, *you* are finite!"

"It seems contradictory," I said defensively.

"Why shouldn't it be contradictory? You're contradictory. I'm contradictory. We are both children of the Universe. Thus it is no surprise that the Universe is contradictory."

"Hawkings says that time can go in either direction just like space, and perhaps when the Universe is contracting some millions of millions of years from now, time may run the other way and we will start our lives by dying, get younger and younger, and then disappear into some womb.

*Hawking, Stephen M., *A Brief History Of Time*, 1988, Bantam.

We will forget the past and remember the future."

He shook his head sadly. "I don't want to be there. I love my memories of the past." He looked dreamy and stroked his tail sensuously.

"Would you like to hear about the anthropic principle?"

He put his chin on his paws and gazed up at me. "Oh yes! Yes!" he whimpered. "*Please* tell me about the anthropic principle!"

"The anthropic principle is that of all the many forms the Universe could have taken (and the mathematicians can conceive of millions of millions of Universe possibilities) the one that really happened is constructed in such a way that it gave birth to intelligent human beings. It has taken ten thousand million years for it to happen, but happen it did. Now there is a Universe which has in it intelligent beings who can ask the question, 'Why is the Universe the way it is?' "

Coyote's jaw dropped and his ears flattened.

I continued, uneasily, "Hawking says the answer to the question 'Why is the Universe the way it is?' is easy; if the Universe had been different, we would not be here."

Coyote sat up and said sternly, "That is the *most disgusting thing I have ever heard!*"

I got defensive again. "So what do you think it was made for — a place for coyotes to stand on and howl?"

He was dignified and huffy. "That's *at least as likely* as the strong anthropic principle!"

"No," I said, "Humans have the ability to comprehend the Universe. Hawking is trying to formulate a Grand Unified Theory of the Universe. He wants to understand what God had in mind. Let me quote:

> There are relatively few [Universes] that would allow for the devel-
> opment of any form of intelligent life. Most sets of values would
> give rise to Universes that, although they might be very beautiful,
> would contain no one to wonder at that beauty.

Coyote was furious! He shook his paw at me. "That's what I hate about churches! You humans go to church and say how wonderful God is, but what you really are saying is how wonderful *you* are; how special you are; how you are the whole culmination of the divine spark. I wouldn't mind if you had a church that just said straight out, 'We humans are It, the best in the Universe!' That would be wrong, but it would be honest. Instead you say, 'Hey can we help it if God created us specially!' You cover up your ego with humble praise of God for making you so damn wonderful that the whole Universe exists for you!"

In as calming a manner as I could muster I said, "I agree with you, Coyote. It *is* human egotism to think we're the best. But, don't you ever wonder *why* the Universe?"

"I don't want to wonder why the Universe!" he yelled. "Not if it means the creature doing the wondering comes to the conclusion that it was designed for him or her personally!"

"So, why the Universe if not to make you and me?"

He squinted at me and spoke slowly; "The god-damn Universe exists because the god-damn Universe wants to exist! It wants to exist so it exists!"

"Gee, Hawking said something like that at the end of his book. Here it is:

> Even if there is only one possible unified theory, it is just a set of rules and equations. What is it that breathes fire into the equations and makes a Universe for them to describe? The usual approach of science of constructing a mathematical model cannot answer questions of why there should be a Universe for the model to describe. Why does the Universe go to all the bother of existing? Is the unified theory so compelling that it brings about its own existence? Or does it need a Creator, and if so, does he have any other effect on the Universe?

Coyote said, "The answer to Hawking's question is that it does not need a creator, and besides, the creator is a mother. The Universe is in fact so compelling, as Hawking says, that it *does* bring itself into being." He sounded certain.

"How can you be so sure that the Universe brings itself into being?"

"You and I are creatures of this Universe. You are human, I am divine. We take part in its nature. Its nature is our nature. We are not apart from it. We create ourselves. So it is reasonable enough for my thinking that the Universe creates itself."

I was puzzled. "We *are* created; we don't create ourselves."

"No! That is a myth that we are created. We create ourselves, you and I. We create a memory of who we were. We create a wish of who we might become. But those don't really exist, except as ideas in the now. Except as neuroses or maybe healthy images which make us either neurotic or healthy in the present. We create ourselves, but not consciously; except once in a great while when we make a rational decision to lose weight or move somewhere healthier. Most of the time we are creating ourselves unconsciously. Just as the Universe does."

I thought about it. I thought, "Makes sense to me." But I wasn't ready to admit it to Coyote. I wondered what Hawking would think.

Coyote interrupted my reveries. "Remember on page 152, Hawking said that by reading the book you increased your brain by two million units; but in terms of entropy, to do that required your using up twenty million million million million units: so just reading the book contributed to the disordering of the Universe by ten million million million times the information you gained. You can see what reading books is doing to the state of the Universe!"

I felt ashamed of causing such damage. Then I realized I was part of the system, so it wasn't lost. It was just changed. I had been creating myself, and the energy for that came from the entropy of the Universe. It seemed exciting to be part of that. I grinned at Coyote. He looked smug.

Then it hit me!

"You mean you'd read the book before you came in here?"

He grinned, showed all his teeth. "You mean you didn't know Stephen Hawking was a coyote?"

I fall into these things every time. I knew I had been tricked.

COYOTE DENIES HE'S A SHADOW; HE THINKS HE'S THE REAL THING.

ut for an early morning walk, I was startled when Coyote slipped from behind a pinon pine and fell in step.

"Where you been? Haven't seen you at the donut shop," he said.

"I've been trying to get a few pounds off before I go east to see my relatives. Staying away from sugar bombs."

"You humans are so strange. By the way, I have a little bone to pick with you."

"Pick away."

"There's talk you've been telling people I'm your shadow side. I'm *not* your shadow side! I'm *me!*"

"No, you're not, Coyote. You don't have any reality outside my imagination, outside my psyche."

He stopped. He looked hurt, angry, incredulous.

"I can't believe you said that!"

"Coyote, I tell people I talk to you. They say they understand — that you are a literary device. I tell them no, you are not a literary device. Now people have come to understand that you are a symbol in my shadow side. In that sense you are real. If you believe in Carl Jung, that is.

"I guess I'm making progress! First I was merely a literary device. Now I am a symbol in your shadow side, and therefore I exist in your mind. Boy, am I grateful and flattered!"

"So, who do *you* think you are?"

He shrugged. "I *think* I am Coyote, a mid-level deity of the North American continent, a manifestation of the divine sense of humor."

"No, Coyote, sorry. We have it on good authority there are no deities, major, minor, or mid-level. It has been clearly demonstrated that what you think you are does not exist. So you have to be my shadow side, a symbol of that part of me that resists being civilized. The part of me it is unwise to show in public."

I had him stumped. I felt good.

"How come you have this shadow side I am part of?"

He had me stumped. "I don't know. I just know everyone has a shadow side."

"You sure take a lot on faith!" He stomped a bug crossing the path.

"Don't stomp that bug!" I said, too late. "That's wanton cruelty."

"I didn't do anything," he said in all innocence. "That was your shadow side stomping the bug."

"Go run through the pines and let me walk in peace!"

Coyote gave me a poke. "You know, you're a nice easy-going guy until your basic unexamined beliefs get challenged. Then you get cranky. I thought you were supposed to be a liberal, open to new ideas."

I *was* getting annoyed. "I don't have any unexamined beliefs!"

"Where did you get this idea that there aren't any gods and I am your shadow side?"

"It's just one of those things everyone knows. Everyone who's educated and intelligent. None of the better sort of people believe in gods anymore."

"So, you just go along with what the majority of the better people believe? Is that it? I'm disappointed in you. I thought I'd find a churchman more open minded than that."

"I am open-minded. We all have open minds and we have open-mindedly figured out that the gods are figments of the human imagination. Including you, my hairy friend."

Coyote reflected. "You haven't told me why you have this shadow side."

"It's an image that seems to explain things."

"Like what?"

"Like why people like me live civilized lives even though we are bored by being civilized. Why civilized people do things they know are uncivilized, but they just can't help doing."

"You think it explains anything to say it's your shadow doing it?"

I was silent. Of course it didn't explain anything, but I was reluctant to admit that.

Coyote spoke. "You want to know the real scoop on this shadow business?"

I knew I was in for it, but what is friendship for? You get to hear what you don't want to hear.

"So, tell me."

"Only a few people know this. You are being punished for what you did in a prior life."

My heart sank. My friend had gone New Age. All those wooden coyotes they sell to the tourists had gone to his head.

"Coyote! Coyote! Knock it off, compadre!"

He looked about wildly. "A vision quest! We need a vision quest!"

He spun around. His eyes rolled back. He fell flat on his back, panting.

"I see it! I see it! I see your former life for which you are being punished."

"Please don't tell me I was Cleopatra."

"No, no, no! Oh, it all makes sense!" He rolled in the dust, laughing and screaming. "Of course! Oh, God, I love it! Oh, what a divine sense of humor God has!" He kicked his heels in the air.

I was embarrassed. What if someone had come along and seen me talking to this hysterical coyote?

"Get up! Get up!"

He cocked an eye at me.

"Still think I'm your imagination?"

"If anyone comes, I'm going to deny I ever knew you."

"You want to hear what it is? You want to know what your former life was for which you are being punished?"

"Yes, yes, but for God's sake get up and get presentable. Little children go to school along this path."

"You . . . you . . . you were a conquistador!"

He roared with laughter and rolled around in the dirt.

Just to humor him and get him calmed down, I said, "Stop laughing and tell me why I am being punished for that?"

He looked at me gravely, but there was a sparkle in his eye. "You did some very bad things as a conquistador. You did them in the name of the Virgin and the King, so you thought that excused you. Very bad things!"

"Things like what?"

He got up and whispered in my ear.

"That bad, eh?"

He nodded and grinned. I grinned, too.

I asked him, "How come *you* don't get punished when you do things like that?"

"I am a mid-level deity. It is part of my work! *You* did it because you wanted to."

He smirked.

"So how am I being punished in this life for my sins as a conquistador in another life!"

He was surprised. "You don't get it?"

"No. I don't consider this life a punishment. I am very happy."

"So, why all this worrying about a shadow side if you're so happy?"

I was beginning to get it.

"You mean I am being punished for my uncivilized behavior in another life by being over-civilized in this life?"

"You're getting it. Not only that, but having committed those crimes in the name of the Virgin and the King, not to mention other hypocritical rationalizations, you have been sentenced by the divine sense of humor to minister to a congregation of rationalists who don't believe in God. *Now* tell me you don't believe in divine justice!"

"Wait a minute—was my being a conquistador a punishment for something else before that?"

"The way it works, you were probably being compensated for a prior misfortune. After all, you enjoyed acting out the shadow side of your soul as a conquistador. Your real offense was rationalizing it all in the name of the Virgin and the King. That sort of thing gives the Queen of Heaven and legitimate government a bad name."

"What was I before I was a conquistador?"

He grinned, sighed, spun around again. His eyes rolled back and his tongue lolled out. He stopped, his eyes came front, and he looked thoughtful.

"You were a heretic burned at the stake in the Inquisition. You ranted in the public square about the riches and corruption of the Pope."

"Coyote, if we packaged this right, we could make a bundle."

"Too late. It's been done."

"Let me see if I've got this straight. I was a heretic burned at the stake. So in compensation I was a conquistador who did uncivilized things. Now I am being punished for that by being a reasonable civilized human being. Is that it?"

"You got it!"

"You are telling me that being a civilized reasonable human being is a punishment in the eyes of the divine sense of humor?"

"You got it!"

"And you are not my shadow side. You are simply nostalgia for the unfettered days of being a conquistador?"

"You got it!"

"Can you tell me what's next after this hell of being civilized, liberal, thoughtful, reflective, reasonable?"

"Remember, Hawking said that for humans time only runs in one direction? You wouldn't be able to believe it even if I told you."

"Do I have to do this all my life, or is there a chance for parole?"

"You'd need a parole plan. I could see about getting it through. After all, I *am* the Trickster!"

"I know, That's what worries me."

"No harm trying. One condition, though. You have to believe in me and give up the idea that I am a figment of your psyche. You have to believe the divine sense of humor is real!"

"Done! I believe in you! Oh, yes! Coyote, I believe in *you*! Get me out of this, Coyote!"

"So what's your plan?" he said.

"My plan is . . . my plan is . . . I'll run for Mayor on the Coyote ticket!"

"It's been done."

"Oh, well . . ." I couldn't think of anything! I couldn't think of anything outrageously uncivilized!

Coyote smiled and disappeared.

I thought, "Well, at least I have a mid-level deity for a friend. Someone who can explain why things are the way they are."

I let myself in the patio door, and my wife asked, "Have a nice walk?"

"Coyote joined me. I found out some interesting things."

"That's nice. How about some tofu and oat-bran for breakfast?"

"Just what I wanted," I said.

COYOTE GOES CAMPING

ith a back-seat full of camping gear, I picked Coyote up in Gallina, N.M. where he had been on personal business. We headed west for Chaco Canyon.

"You brought the donuts?" he asked.

"Two dozen."

"Two dozen? We've got two days ahead of us!"

"You know, Coyote, I took my son and stepson camping once. I got them each a dozen candy bars for six days. One son ate all twelve in the first two hours; the other made them last the six days."

"I can see which one took after you."

"Go easy, Coyote. 'I yam what I yam,' as Popeye used to say."

"But *I'm* who you'd like to be!" He grinned with friendly malice.

"Some days, Coyote, some days. Which is why we are going to Chaco Canyon to camp. Get away from the city and the telephone. Get out where we can see the stars and not wash and get some relief from civilization."

"Why don't you become a hermit in the desert?"

"Oh, I found I can only stand my own company about 24 hours. Then I have to be with people. I can stand people for three or four days; then I have to get by myself and let my head clear. Find myself again. It's hard to be in touch with myself when I am paying attention to other people. I go back and forth between company and aloneness. Now that I figured that out, it works well."

"What do you do when you are alone?"

"Soak up the scenery. Listen to music. Talk to myself."

He rummaged in the back seat for the donuts. With his mouth full, he asked, "How can you talk to yourself? I don't understand that."

"I have come to realize I am many people. There's the child who remembers long summer days with buttercups and fireflies, who wishes those days would come again. There's my adolescent who thinks sex is all there is. There's my idealistic minister persona who hopes the world could be better. Then there's you who wants to take the world as it is now and revel in it, rejoice in it. All my personalities can manage many conversations."

"I told you before not to think of me as part of you," he said with a touch of indignation. "I exist in my own right. I am not a figment of your imagination."

"I fully understand how you feel. I am glad to give you credence as a deity who existed long before I did and will continue to exist after I am gone. Still, I admit you into my selfhood and accept you as part of my selfhood. Therefore you are part of me, quite apart from your separate existence."

He grinned. "It is confusing, isn't it?"

"It always has been," I answered happily. "And do you consider me a part of your imagining?"

"Why, what a nice idea," he exclaimed. "I've never thought of you that way. Yes," he said emphatically, "*I* made *you* up!"

"Thank you! I've always wondered how I came to be. Not physically, I mean, but spiritually."

"It was that chance encounter at Ghost Ranch," he said. "We became aware of each other, and we created each other. That's the way of all relationships," he added, matter-of-factly.

"You think there is no separateness, no uniqueness?"

"We're all separate and unique. But at the same time we are created by each other and create each other. You made decisions about work and who you married and having children. You thought those were creative acts. They were. They created you. They were irrevocable. So here you are, created by the people with whom you have had a creative relationship. You were even created by those who rejected you, especially back there when your mother wouldn't buy you donuts slathered in sugar. Or when you were divorced, or when your children went through adolescence. All that created you."

I thought about it for awhile.

"You mean I didn't have much to do with it?"

"You had lots to do with it. You accepted some of it and rejected some of it. You ignored some things that could have bothered you and were unhappy about what you thought you didn't get. It's all part of the big ball of wax of being a person."

"Then I had to run into a Trickster deity instead of Jesus in the garden, 'where the joys we share as we tarry there, none other has every known!' "

"If I'd known that's what you wanted, I wouldn't have come on this camping trip."

"I prefer being in the desert with a Coyote than in the garden with Jesus. But that's not a judgement. That's just a personal preference."

"So that's why you found me instead of him. We were both there waiting to be found."

We were bounding along a desert gravel road with the wind in our faces, and all was right with the world.

"Stop at this store," he said suddenly. "We need donuts."

"You ate the whole two dozen?"

"No, there's two left. But that's not enough for the weekend. You're not expecting me to chase road-runners for food, are you? It's a vacation."

We stopped and got two large sacks of day-old donuts and tied them on top of the camping equipment.

The ranger at the entrance to Chaco Canyon National Park looked hard at Coyote and said, "Keep him on a leash!" Coyote was incensed. He stood up on the seat and said, "*Do what?*" She was a little intimidated, but she was a modern woman doing her bureaucratic duty. She stared right back at him and said to him, not me, "All dogs must be kept on a leash no longer than six feet."

Coyote got histrionic. He clapped one paw to his furry chest and stretched the other to the sky.

"Madam, I am not a domesticated *dog*!"

"I don't care who you are! You look canine to *me*, and you stay on a leash while you're in the park. Or you're *out*!"

I popped the clutch and we were gone, Coyote speechless with rage. He sputtered. He cursed. He looked back at the ranger booth with murder in his eye. He was still mad as we unpacked the car at the campground.

"You better not have a leash in all this stuff," he said darkly.

"Have no fear, but when the ranger drives by, lie under the car."

"I'm going to organize the poodles in this campground, and we're going to raise hell all night!"

"Coyote, compadre, if you were just a coyote you could do that. But you're Coyote, and you have certain social obligations, just like me and the ranger-woman. Calm down, and I'll get supper ready."

He sulked. He played with the Coleman lantern and broke it. He tried to get some rock music on the radio. It was like having a 13-year-old along. When I opened the cans of chili, he exploded:

"Wolf brand chili? You would eat chili made from *wolves*? That's awful! I won't have it!"

"Calm *down*! It's the name of the people who make the chili. It's not made of wolves; it's made of old cows."

After supper we went to the campfire to hear Ranger Claude tell about the people who lived in Chaco Canyon before the Anasazi came.

"I used to know them," said Coyote. "They were good people."

"Please don't tell Ranger Claude," I said.

Ranger Claude mentioned that the basket-weavers occasionally ate groundhogs. He added that when he himself had been a boy growing up in Ohio in the Depression, sometimes his father shot a groundhog so there would be meat on the table. Coyote told Ranger Claude that he liked groundhog too. Ranger Claude asked him how he cooked it, and Coyote said he ate them raw. Ranger Claude looked like he was glad the tourist season was about over.

"That Ranger Claude is a good ol' boy," said Coyote on the way back to the campground. "Maybe we could make groundhog chili and sell it in Santa Fe as natural and cholesterol-free."

"It would probably work. People in Santa Fe will eat anything they've never heard of before."

We sat by the campfire, looked at the stars, and Coyote sang a little. He sang about the wonder of the universe and the joys of being Coyote. Some poodles did join in. It was a pleasant evening of canine company, with no human cares. I did find coyotes are no fun to sleep with. They smell bad and dream restlessly. I left the tent and slept under the stars.

In the morning when the ranger came by, Coyote lay under the car in an imitation of the best ol' dog you ever saw. I complimented him.

After breakfast we snooped around the ruins, and then we climbed to the mesa top. We looked down on Pueblo Bonito. We were silent. Then I spoke what I was feeling.

"It's sort of sad and sort of moving to see the ruins people leave. They worked so hard, and all that's left are ruins. But because they worked so hard and left ruins, we remember them. We know at least they existed. They weren't completely swept away by the sands of the desert and the sands of time."

"We don't leave ruins."

"And people don't remember you a thousand years later."

"So what? Who wants to be remembered?"

"We humans can't imagine not existing. We want to exist at least in someone's memory. Or leave a monument that someone will find a thousand years later and say, 'Some clever folks lived here.'"

"So what? If you're not alive to appreciate their wonder at the monument you left for them, what good does the monument do?"

"It's psychological, Coyote, an emotional thing. I admit it isn't reasonable. People want to be remembered, so they build monuments. They have to make their mark in the earth, even if it's only carving an aspen. It's part of being human; the persistence of being."

"The point of being alive is to be alive! Why do people waste their lives constructing a monument so people will remember them when they're dead? They could have put that energy into having a good time or making life better for the human race. Or for coyotes, for that matter, like you do."

"It's called *ego*, Coyote. I have been reading some heavy sociology about the stages people go through. When they're little, they are child-like. They don't have all this ego. They take life as it comes, as you say they should. Then they get to a stage when they have to differentiate between self and parents. They start to develop an ego. Which is fun! It means I am I. I do not exist just as an extension of my mother or my clan; *I* exist! And so I want to leave my mark on the earth; maybe on the Universe."

"Maybe ego is what is wrong with humans. Maybe that's why you were evicted from the garden way back there."

"You could be right. Which may be why in later life, people become aware that life and goodness and beauty transcend the human ego. In later years they get some child-likeness back, but at a more sophisticated level. They see the whole thing and appreciate it and understand it and don't have the emotional need to carve their initials in it anymore. They can just accept it as a wondrous happening, a gift."

"Well said!"

We headed down the trail. A song flashed in my head, and I sang it for Coyote.

> "We are traveling in the footsteps
> Of those who've gone before,
> But we'll all be reunited
> On a new and distant shore."

We appeared in the parking lot singing:

> "When the saints go marching in,
> O, when the saints go marching in;
> O, Lord, I want to be in that number
> When the saints go marching in!"

A tourist in plaid shorts got us on her video camera. We were memorialized for an audience back home, wherever that might be.

We came home the long way through the Navajo reservation. Coyote popped a tape in the deck, and *Der Rosenkavelier* assaulted the silence of the desert. We hardly spoke for an hour; just admiring the badlands.

Coyote asked, totally out of the blue, "Do you believe in God?"

"I believe in you, you're a god."

"No, you're ducking the question. I mean do you believe in Big Mama in the Sky?"

"I have always answered that question by saying some days I do and some days I don't."

"Fair enough. You're only human."

"How about you? Do you believe in Big Mama in the Sky?"

"Of course! How could I not believe in my own Mama?"

"Oh."

He grinned slyly. "Now I've got you! You claim I am part of you. So if I am part of you, and I believe in Big Mama in the Sky, then that means that at least a part of *you* believes in Big Mama in the Sky!"

"You are telling me that if I don't believe in Big Mama in the Sky, I can't believe in you?"

"Right!"

It was lovely and we were in magnificent country. I was totally free of my rational reservations. I yelled,

"Yes, Coyote! I believe! I believe!"

"Hallelujah, brother! I knew I'd bring you round."

As we came back through Gallina, I asked if he were getting out. He said, no he was going on to Coyote, which is the name of the next town. As he got out in front of the Coyote bar, a child with a rather long nose and premature beard said,

"Where you been, Coyote?"

"In church," he said, and they walked off hand in hand.

COYOTE WANTS TO KNOW WHY
WE HONOR VETERANS

oyote came into the study carrying a bag of donuts.

"What are you doing in your study?" he asked. "It's Veterans' Day. Why aren't you taking the day off? I expected you to be down at the donut shop swapping war stories."

"My war stories all took place in Tiajuana. I can't tell them and keep my respected place in the community."

He offered the donuts. I rummaged in the bag.

"There are no oat-bran muffins in there, Reverend. It's a holiday. Pretend you're back in Tiajuana and have a jelly-filled. I'll never tell."

You have to humor the Trickster in your life, or there will be trouble. So I took a jelly-filled donut, bit into it, and its filling went all down my shirtfront.

"Ha, ha," said Coyote.

"Ha, ha, yourself, furry friend."

I took a new donut from the bag, aimed it at him and squeezed. He had lemon all down his furry front. He grabbed for the bag, but fortunately for my study that was the last donut.

"I'll get you!" He grinned maliciously and licked his coat. I dabbed ineffectively with my handkerchief at my shirt front.

"Sounds like war!" I said.

"War I don't understand," he said. "A good food fight between friends, or an insult match for the fun of it; those I can understand. It's part of a robust friendship. But war? Why would you go off and kill someone you don't even know?"

"Would you kill someone you know?"

"Makes more sense. Most murders are between people who know each other. Wives shooting husbands; that sort of thing. That's understandable. That's being human. Even animals get angry at their mates and children occasionally. Even the gods get bored with their lovers. It is understandable to harbor resentment and murderous thoughts about your loved ones. But go out and kill *strangers?*"

I gave up on the jelly on my shirt. I envied him the ability to lick himself clean. I knew I was being set up, but I decided to play it straight.

"It's simple, Coyote. Our government says, 'Those people over there are your enemy. They want to kill you. You have to kill them first.' So all the able-bodied men are drafted. You just go do it. It's part of a man's life."

"You could get killed yourself."

"True, but people try not to think that thought. What humans cannot control, they tend not to think about."

"Story of my life. Things are always out of control, especially where roadrunners are concerned."

"Exactly. You never think of the consequences to yourself when you are setting up a roadrunner trap."

"True. But I can rise from the dead. You can't. So it's different. I can afford to be stupid."

"We humans are beginning to realize that. In the old days the government encouraged the myth that the happy warrior goes right to Valhalla upon dying in battle. Our culture doesn't believe that any more, so the fun has gone out of being a dead hero."

"Why would people have believed that?" He was genuinely puzzled. Coyote is a here-and-now deity.

"There are many theories. One is that the kings encourage the priests to encourage the people to believe there is a higher purpose to war. Another theory is that civilization is so dull that men need a war occasionally so they can indulge in rape and pillage. Probably both theories are correct."

"Wars are a function of civilization?"

"It seems that way. The more advanced the nations, the more efficient and barbaric are its tools of war. We have reached the height of civilization by inventing weapons that eliminate the inefficiency of needing soldiers. We can wipe out a large nation in an hour or so while getting wiped out ourself. Those who don't get wiped out will have an ecologically ruined planet. It is a trick worthy of yourself, old Trickster."

Coyote looked demure. "Well, we gods had something to do with that. The threat was so bad that we had to intervene. Los Alamos and Rocky Flats are part of the divine stop-gap measure to save the planet by instituting the terror of mutually assured destruction.

"I have heard that theory put forth by some Los Alamos people, but I have never had it confirmed by anyone of your stature."

We both laughed, and I am still not sure whether he was pulling my leg. You never can tell when a deity is telling the truth. Maybe the nuclear stand-off was part of the divine plan to save the planet.

"If war is now an anachronism," Coyote persisted, "why do you still honor veterans?"

"Veterans' Day is an anachronism itself. There won't be any surviving veterans of the next big war. I remember the excitement of World War II when I was a kid. I also remember my mother's pain. She was asked to unveil the war memorial on the village green because she had three sons in World War II. She refused the honor because she thought that even if war was necessary, it was still evil. When the government requested my services in the Korean War I was less than enthusiastic. Though it turned out to be quite interesting since the process transformed me from a rather innocent small-town boy to a Marine."

"Where you proud to be a veteran afterward?"

"Not in the sense that I had done something noble. Personally the experience was good for me. I made some good friends, got away from home. I came home a lot wiser. I'm sure that isn't what the government had in mind, but that's what happened."

"What about the killer instinct? I don't see you as a killer."

"Thanks. I was never forced to confront the possibility. I was trained to be a killer. I was trained that I and my unit had a duty to survive. That was a duty I could heartily go along with. I like surviving. Yet my religious training and my adult value system would have been severely traumatized if I had had to kill another human being. I used to hunt as a kid, but I gave it up when I encountered a dying animal. I don't know, Coyote. I was never tested, and I'm glad I never was."

"Well, then how *can* people be trained to be killers?"

"Mostly the killer has to told that the people he is supposed to kill are less than human. It is hard for a human to kill a human on a human-to-human basis. The enemy has to be de-humanized. That's what propaganda is for."

"Have you succeeded in de-humanizing yourselves in the nuclear age?"

"That's the odd thing. Coyote. It may be another trick of the gods, but I think people are becoming more aware of the humanity of our potential enemies. And of course it will not be just 'them' that are killed; it will also be 'us and our.'"

"And *us*, too," Coyote said sternly. "Don't forget the other species are here."

"Good point! I suppose the whole human race could agree to specie-suicide, but we can't depersonalize the other species. Maybe the term should be 'de-animalize'!"

"How about you? Are you a pacifist now?"

"Yes and no," I said. "Yes, because I believe war in even the most righteous cause is always tragic. Maybe it has to be, but it is always tragic. Yes, because war always dehumanizes the enemy and dehumanizes those trained to kill. Yes, because war is always the result of a failure of politics. In fact wars are politics—the powerful using the powerless as pawns. The presidents and generals stay where it's safe after they have declared war. Wars mean the leaders couldn't be bothered with intelligent humane agreements. Vietnam and the Berlin Wall didn't have to happen; they were not inevitable. So I *am* a pacifist personally and as a matter of political principle. I do not wish to glorify war by word or example. Perhaps I am in the minority, but I think war is always a matter of shame."

"But you also said 'no' to being a pacifist."

"The human world is a dangerous place, Coyote. There is a sort of pacifism that would not resist evil. There is the quietism and resignation that accepts fascism. I couldn't take that attitude. Now we see the people of the Soviet Union and eastern Europe defiant, alive, happy, tearing down the fascist institutions. That's revolution, Coyote. It's dangerous. The tanks cleared Tianenmen Square while the world watched. Those people put human dignity on the line and paid with their lives."

"So you are a pacifist when it suits you, and a warrior when it suits you?"

"Only way to live, my furry friend! If the government doesn't like it, too bad for the government. If the ideological conservatives don't like it, too bad for them. If the ideological radicals don't like it, too bad for them. You said it, Coyote. A pacifist when it suits me and a warrior when it suits me. But not just when it suits *me*, Coyote. When it suits my humanity! Not as a matter of convenience, but as a matter of my soul."

"Maybe you think wars and Veterans' Day are things of the past?"

"Probably not, but I am more optimistic than I was twenty years ago. What is happening is what Marshall McLuhan and others predicted; the electronic media are making the planet a global village. We're seeing we are all human and all in it together. Tough on the careerist politicians of the super-powers and the little countries. Maybe war *is* too terrible to have wars. Maybe the world knows too much to let the leaders get away with what they have gotten away with. I am optimistic, Coyote."

"It's a great trick!" said the Great Trickster. "What if the American people followed the example of the Soviet people and decided not to follow the rules set up by the elite for the good of the elite?"

"Hush, Coyote. That's commie talk and this is Veterans' Day. Commie talk is not allowed on Veterans' Day."

"Then I have a suggestion," he said. "There is a rally on the Plaza organized by some uppity women. What say we cruise down there and pick up some chicks?"

"Coyote, I am a married man with a dignified esteemed position in the community. I cannot go to a rally to pick up chicks."

"So I'll go by myself. Thanks for the conversation."

"The women at the rally are not the sort to get picked up, friend."

"You never can tell. Even coyotes get lucky sometimes!"

He disappeared, and I went home and looked at an old photo of myself in Marine dress blues. I said to myself,

"You've come a long way, baby!"

Coyote Wants To Know What Money Will Buy

ore and more I stay away from the donut shop. I am part of the new American Puritanism that puts longevity before pleasure. However, I needed to talk with Coyote, so I steeled myself and went there. I sat down, ordered a donut, and Coyote materialized beside me. He said he'd have a dozen; six lemon and six raspberry-filled.

"I need to talk to you," I said. "The people at my church are concerned about money. I need to come up with a good rationale for mentioning the unmentionable in church."

"Don't ask me! I don't have pockets. I wait for you to buy the donuts."

"I don't know much about money either. But I'm talking about money as a spiritual issue, an emotional issue. You being spiritual, I thought you might have some ideas."

Inhaling a donut in one bite, he said, "We can wonder together as long as your money holds out!"

"I suppose this is tax-deductible." I said, "I can see the IRS reading it; 'three dozen donuts for Coyote, sermon preparation.'"

"So what is this tax stuff? I can never get anyone to play this time of the year. They're all in shock about their taxes. It's as though the whole country has been to a funeral."

"Taxes are simple. Taxes are a socialist scheme to provide employment for accountants. Sort of like the Pentagon which produces jet fighters for boys who are bored with street racing."

Coyote looked at me with admiration. "You are coming along as a coyote cynic! Keep working on it! You have great spiritual potential!"

I blushed modestly and signaled for another round of donuts. I knew what he meant. One must have a conversion experience to become a mystic, whether Zen, Christian, or coyote. One of the pleasures of being a neophyte mystic is to play games with the standard cultural answers. Stand them on their head. See if that makes more sense. For example, consider the truth that people buy cars so they can go places. Turn it over; people go places so they will have a reason to buy a car. A revelation. A deeper truth. Coyote and I are now close enough that we each know the other knows this.

"So," says he, "can we apply this principle to money?"

"I am slow this morning. Please expand on that."

"One does not need money to survive." Coyote said. "Animals survive without money. Your primitive humans survived without money. The pueblo people and the plains people met and swapped things — pots for hides. Even today most people could survive on a lot less than they think they could. They might feel underprivileged doing it, but that is a spiritual disease, feeling underprivileged."

"But people need money to buy stuff. It's obvious, Coyote."

"That's because you live in a money-culture and have been taught that it's obvious. Jesus said, 'behold the lilies of the field, they neither toil nor spin, yet Solomon in all his glory was not arrayed as one of these.' "

"I must not be spiritually advanced enough to appreciate that. Lilies and humans are different."

"That's what humans think! Humans think they are more blessed of God. Or more despised by God. Whichever, it's *ego, ego, ego*! Let go of it!"

"Not til the day I die!"

"Then you'll want a band and a Cadillac hearse. Can you *afford* it?"

Spitefully, I said, "I'll save up for it!" He was getting to me. All these donuts and no help.

"Why do *you* thinks humans use money," I asked.

"From my observations, humans buy things to show they've got money. After they've bought the things, they don't have the money. So they really buy things to show they have money left over after they have everything they want. People who live on subsistence can't play the game. You have to have money over and above what you need, or be able to pretend you do to play the game."

"You can use a credit card," I said ruefully.

"That's just borrowing someone else's money to pretend it's yours.

That seems to be a national habit."

"Ben Franklin *does* seem un-American."

Looking me in the eye, he said, "According to what I've seen there are many money games you humans play. Some are healthy, some are unhealthy. Some of them are spiritually nutritious, sort of whole-wheat oat-bran money games. And some are like these donuts; delicious, but in the long run unhealthy."

"Tell me about the unhealthy ones first."

"The unhealthy ones are games involving taking up more space than one human needs. Using more of the earth's resources than one human needs. Using money to control other people's lives, other people's spirits. Using money to buy people and exploit people."

"Hush, Coyote, you're talking like a Communist again," I glanced around furtively.

"It isn't a matter of capitalism or communism. A capitalist company can be managed in a humane way. In fact it will probably be more successful if it treats its employees and customers as humans. This isn't a matter of -isms. This is a matter of human spiritual growth. Will you humans play healthy games with your money or psychologically destructive games? This country of yours has seemed more exploitative in the past decade, and as a consequence has become less healthy. Over in the Soviet Union, the Russian wolves tell me, the leaders forgot the people and now their system is dying of rot."

"Then what are some healthy money games?"

"Investments in people are always healthy money games. Remember the G.I. Bill? It did more to make America a good place to live than all the armaments industries put together. It was a national investment in educating people. I'll bet maybe a quarter or a third of your congregation got some of their education from the G.I. Bill."

"Certainly I did," I said. "Even today my youngest son is spending a year after high school in a program that will give him experience and skills in community organizing. I think that's a good investment in youth."

"Wow! They're training him to be a coyote? This country needs some smart trained young coyotes! This country with its fat, complacent, self-centered population that has given up on the democratic process, given up on caring for life's losers, given up on idealism and community and commonwealth."

I was stunned. Incredulous, I asked, "You mean you *care*?"

He was embarrassed. His cover had slipped. He reached over and ate my donut while he collected himself. Then he whispered, so the other coyotes couldn't hear:

"Yes, I care! You humans hold the future of the planet in your hands. I wish it weren't so, but it is. I have to wish you well because I am part of the commonwealth of life on this planet. That's the only reason I talk to you. I look at your congregation and I think maybe there's hope!"

I was moved. Coyote, the Trickster god, thought some modest little churches were a hope for the commonwealth of planetary life? It seemed like a tall mission for a small band.

He went on. "The reason I think congregations like yours are a hope for the future is that you are open to new ideas. All your human churches try to be places where the spirit can grow, but most of them are locked into ancient ways of seeing the world, which aren't appropriate now that we're running out of maneuvering room. Not long ago I read that Statement of Purposes you have in the foyer from the Unitarian Universalist denomination. You affirm the importance of the inherent worth and dignity of every person, not the subservience of humans to the gods, not the inferiority of some people to other people. You affirm justice, equity, compassion. You affirm a free and responsible search for truth. You affirm democracy and the goal of world peace. Not many other churches affirm those values. You even respect what you call the inter-dependent web of all existence. I think if the animals ever came to church, they'd come to your church."

"We've got one coyote — you — and some church mice. We could make the others welcome." Then I paused and gathered my thoughts. "We've strayed from our original subject of money games."

"Not so," said Coyote. "When you humans place your bets with your discretionary money, you put your money where your spirit is. Which is why I worry about some of your members . . ."

"They probably give generously to other good causes," I said, defensively.

"They probably do, but so what? We are talking sources of the spiritual life. There are lots of wonderful, worthwhile organizations doing good things, but they are not specialists in the meaning of life. As I see them, your human churches focus on meanings. Other churches say the meanings come "down" from God. Your church says there are many sources of spiritual meaning. The direct experience of transcending mystery. That's one we other animals like to do. The second source of spiritual meaning you honor are the words and deeds of prophetic women and men who confront the structure of evil with compassion and justice and love. That is very human. We animals don't do that because we don't have structures of evil. You celebrate the tools of justice, compassion and love by which you can overcome your own humanly created evil. The devil doesn't *make* you do evil, you know. You choose it. Maybe for psychologically sick and neurotic reasons, but you choose it. And people of compassion and love and justice can *choose* to try to undo it. You honor the religious prophets."

He was silent, gazing into the mirror behind the counter.

"You honor all the world's religions. Amazing! You could be proud of that. You don't condemn people with different gods. Instead, you see if you can learn from them more about the transcending mystery. All those varied pictures of the gods are insights into how humans experience the mystery. Your people are willing to listen and be taught. As a minor deity, I admire that."

"Your church says the way to respond to God's love for us is to love your fellow humans. When you get love, pass it on! Spend it! Like money! Don't hoard it! Put the love you receive to work by investing it in other people. That's what we deities do and you humans used to do before you were civilized."

"Your church also affirms, the glory of humanity which is science. We animals are sceptical about your science; it has brought some really bizarre things to pass. But we admire your passion to know and explore and study and understand. If there was one human characteristic we might like to have, it is that unfailing curiosity. Yours is the only church I know that respects science as science rather than fearing science will erode religious authority."

I was overwhelmed. I had no idea the Trickster knew so much about religion.

"You know," he said reflectively, "I wish I had some money so I could contribute to your church."

"You already have. The congregation loves to hear what you have to say."

"Talk's cheap."

I was silent.

"That was a joke."

I nodded.

"What do you do with the children?" he asked. "I hope you don't sit them down in little rooms and have adult humans tell them the Truth."

"No, this Sunday they are going to plant a tree."

"Damn! That's nice!"

It was time to go. Coyote flashed a five-dollar bill.

"I'm buying!"

"*You* are buying *my* donuts?"

"Right! I found the five dollars in the street this morning. As your poet Walt Whitman said, he finds letters from God in the streets and leaves them there because there will always be more. Most of the good stuff we get in life we probably don't deserve, so we might as well spend it. Pass it on. Besides I believe in donuts for preachers so they are fat and unhealthy and happy."

We slid off the donut shop stools.

"Coyote, I wish you'd come tell my congregation what you've told me."

"They'd never take my word for it. The question is whether they believe it themselves. If they don't, things are worse than I thought."

So now you know what Coyote would buy if Coyote had any money.

COYOTE WANTS TO KNOW WHY HUMANS USED TO THINK GOD WAS MALE

od's in Her heaven, all's right with the world! I thought to myself. Then a small voice asked,

"Are you busy?"

There is a grey snout and two yellow eyes looking in the door.

"Coyote, compadre," I said, "Come in, come in."

Then I realize it is not Coyote.

"Oh! I thought you were someone else. Excuse me!"

"It's perfectly okay," she said, and came in. "I can understand the mistake. I am Doña Coyote. I am Wile E. Coyote's significant other."

"Charmed!" I said, "Delighted!"

"May I?" she asked, and hopped up on my sofa. "I wanted to have a little chat. I'm not sure what's happening with Wile E. I thought perhaps you could shed some light."

"I will be glad to try."

I wondered where my loyalties lay. I knew my friend wasn't perfect. I feel an obligation to whomever needs an honest counselor. I centered myself, as all good Santa Fe counselors do, and let myself go with the flow.

"*Why* are you filling his head with all this god-talk?"

She was calm, but she spoke with great feeling. I lost my center. I was tense.

"He used to run with the pack, howl in harmony with his fellows, help around the den occasionally, bring home a rodent or two. Now he talks about god all the time. He wonders whether howling at the moon actually *accomplishes* anything besides making him feel better and promoting community among coyotes. I ask him, 'What's wrong with feeling better and promoting community among coyotes?' He says it isn't enough.

Does the moon *hear* him? Does the moon *care* that coyotes are howling their prayers to her? Can the moon really do anything about what is happening to the planet? Or is it all a delusion in the heads of coyotes?" Her eyes filled. "He thinks you're his friend, but as far as I can see, he's just getting fat on donuts and thinking more than is good for a coyote."

She continued, "I'm just a simple coyote. I know he's the Trickster. He loves his profession, and he's *good* at it. That's fine for him. I am just a simple coyote."

She looked at me to see how I was taking it. I remained bland and open.

"He's a good lover and a good conversationalist. He cares about all sorts of creatures, including you humans. Which is more than I can say for myself! He enjoys life! So do I! We have a lot of fun together, and we have the respect of the other coyotes. We have a good life. I enjoy teaching the kits their predator skills. Life makes sense to me *just the way it is!* You work hard, keep your nose clean, have some fun, good loving, a monthly group howl at the goddess in the moon; what more does anyone *need*? But ol' Wile E.; he's got to lie there *thinking*, trying to puzzle out whether the Universe has a purpose."

"I guess what really got to me was his coming home last Sunday and telling me you talked about whether God was a woman or a man, and how that has all been a big political issue in human history. That was the last straw. I said, 'Wile E. Coyote, you stay away from that place! That's the most stupid non-issue I have ever heard of. How can a specie possibly think they are made in God's image? What conceit! What stupidity! What spiritual corn-syrup! Wile E. Coyote, you are too smart an animal to fall for that stuff. I am ashamed of you, much as I love you.'"

She hesitated. She wasn't tricking me. She took a tissue and dabbed her eyes. She continued.

"You know what he said to me? You know what he *said*?"

I shook my head.

"He said, 'Right, you and I know that's foolish. *We* know God has a furry face and yellow eyes and a long snout. Right?' Naturally I said, 'Of course we know that. All our friends know that. How come humans don't know that?'"

She turned her face away and snuffled into the tissue. I waited. She composed herself. With a certain resignation, she said,

"Then! Then! You know what he said? He had the gall to say to *me*, his significant other, 'Well, aren't we being specie specific, specie chauvinist just as much as the humans?' I tell you I was *shocked*!"

In a very sad voice, she said, "I said, 'Wile E. Coyote, you know you were brought up to believe God has a long furry nose and yellow eyes. *I* was brought up to think God has a long furry nose and yellow eyes. God *has* a long furry nose and yellow eyes, Coyote! That's all there is to it! Why would anyone think God could be a woman or a man? It's *ridiculous*, Coyote, and *I won't stand for it!*' "

She glared at me with her yellow eyes. Her long snout trembled with indignation.

"It's all *your* fault! I wish the Indians had kept Santa Fe. At least *they* have a little respect for the rest of us. *They* have a little humility!

She jumped down from the sofa and addressed me politely, but coldly:

"Thank you for your time. I needed to get it off my chest. He's a good guy despite his tricks. I love him and he loves me, and we have fun together. I just wish he'd stay away from you humans and your totally weird ideas about what's important."

With that she disappeared. I thought I might have imagined the whole thing, but I felt the sofa and there was a warm spot where she'd been.

My benevolent mood was shattered. I needed to clear my head and get centered again. There is nothing like a ride with the top down to bring back the feeling that God's in Her heaven and all's right with the world. I was barely out of the city limits when Coyote materialized beside me.

"Couldn't resist the yellow car with my favorite spinner of theological conundrums!" he yelled. He hit me on the back so hard the car swerved, caught the shoulder, spun around, and kept going in the original direction.

"Hey, hey, hey! Fun!"

"Fun?" I yelled back. "Coyote, you almost got us killed. Then we might have found out a few answers; answers I can wait to find out."

"Curiosity killed the cat," he said smugly. "Say, do you suppose the cat had a theological curiosity about seeing whether the face of God is feline?"

"Ask a cat! Satisfaction brought it back!"

"That's the trouble with cats," he said. "They are so smug about dying and coming back to life with the answers. If you ask them a theological question, they just look as though they have the answer, but you are too dumb to understand the answer if they were to tell you. That's why I do not like cats."

"I know some humans like that. I even know some coyotes like that."

"Uh-oh! I wonder who *you*'ve been talking to!"

"No problem, Coyote. As significant others go, she's a winner. It's just that some creatures imagine there are theological problems and some creatures can't imagine any theological problems. Never the twain shall have meaningful discussions, at least not on theological problems."

Coyote shrugged, and at 40 miles an hour folded down the windshield.

"Let's catch some bugs in our teeth," he grinned.

I caught one on my glasses and pulled off the road. I put the windshield back up, wiped my glasses, and said with a certain desperation:

"Coyote, we must talk."

"We always do. What about?"

"I am perhaps leading you astray, leading you into territory where coyotes are not supposed to be, territory reserved for the humans with the big brain."

"Aw, c'mon. What's wrong with a coyote stretching his brain a little? You think we don't have a brain and a soul and some spiritual sensitivity? Just because you humans are psychologically constipated by co-dependence on God doesn't make you spiritually superior."

"Coyote, compadre, what I am worried about is that all this theology is spoiling you as a coyote."

"Look," he said in his most beguiling male-bonding conspiratorial tone, "Doña Coyote, she's okay. I know she thinks you're a bad influence on me, and probably you are. I'm a bad influence on you, and your wife probably has a few things to say about me. So, buddy, let us not worry about it. It all evens out in the fullness of eternity."

I was being seduced, gladly.

"What our significant others think is no more important than that yucca in bloom," he said. "In fact, the yucca in bloom is more important than, say, the Dow-Jones, which humans take so seriously they go for their guns when it falls. Everyone is crazy, so why should we not also be crazy and fill our idle hours with theological speculation?"

Sitting in an old car on a desert road talking to a coyote, I felt vulnerable about judging what was or was not important. I put the windshield down again, and we moved, though at a slower speed. I had a deep feeling of peace that the world was made for coyotes to have fun in. Ah, I thought, here we can live for the moment!

"Right!" said Coyote. I have gotten used to his reading my mind. Sometimes it seems as though he lives in it, but as he has told me, that is my fantasy.

"I think your significant other, Doña Coyote, is right! I think she is a wise female. I think she is an antidote to our male proclivity to strut and posture and assume larger glories than are called for by reality."

"May I quote you?"

"You may quote me."

"Now," he said, "while we are travelling this desert road that goes nowhere, but passes through magnificent scenery getting there, let us indulge, just the two of us, in the secret sin of theological speculation."

"I'll never tell a soul."

He stuck his tongue out at me. We laughed, and the poor old VW went off the road, down an arroyo, up an embankment, and back on the road.

"God watches over fools," he said.

"Then we're safe in her arms."

"So," he said, serious, "Why *did* humans think of God as a man back before the theologians proclaimed God as dead and the feminist theologians proclaimed the goddess? Why did people of both sexes think it was significant for God to have a penis?"

"It is not usually put that way, Coyote. God is usually described as an old man with a beard."

"Penis, beard; they go together."

"Maybe it was because people thought creating the universe required a lot of heavy lifting."

"A good theory. I like it."

"Yet a lot of women do heavy lifting, too. In some cultures they haul the water and firewood as well as have babies. Which leaves the men free to lie around and tell stories about God."

"So, maybe men are smarter than women and get women to do their work for them; thus giving men the leisure to think up theological rationales for that being the way it is supposed to be."

"That's another good theory."

We drove along, frustrating the bugs who couldn't find any windshield to make a heroic gesture on. It was fun because you could see any large bug coming and take evasive action. We evaded separate bugs at the same time and knocked heads. We were laughing so hard we had to pull over and get out. We stood by the road puddling the dust.

"One unarguable superiority of being male," he said.

"There's not much else to hold onto in the gathering era of male inferiority."

We sniggered. It was good there was no one there to overhear.

Coyote said, "Maybe men made god in their image because they felt so inferior in their bodies compared to what women do with theirs."

"Another good theory, compadre!"

"Why is there this change? Why are we promoting the goddess, going forward to the paleolithic?"

"The negatives for women in having God be male are obvious. But there are negatives for men in being made in the image of God. Men have to be god-like. They can't be gentle or tender or kind. They have to enforce the ways of the system instead of baking a cake for their significant other."

"I have a question," he said. "Does it do any good to howl at the moon?"

"Of course it does! It makes coyotes feel better and it promotes community among coyotes."

"I know *that*. I mean, does it do any good in the sense that the goddess hears and responds and things get better?"

"Of course it does," I said emphatically. "Of course it does! Why do you think things are getting better?"

"And what does God look like?" he asked.

"Well, in the first place She's got a long furry snout and yellow eyes!"

"May I quote you?"

"You may quote me!"

There was silence in the desert as we considered this theophany; that someone like Doña Coyote was god.

"You know what this means, Coyote? This means we're off the hook!"

We put up the windshield, made a u-turn, and with wild yells headed at top speed into town to the donut shop and blessed oblivion.

COYOTE GOES TO A WEDDING

xiting from The Bishop's Lodge, I stopped for the stop sign. Coyote stepped out of the bushes and got in the car.

"What have you been doing at a fancy hostelry like this?" he demanded as the old VW grudged up the hill.

"I was officiating at a wedding."

"Officiating? You mean you were being officious?"

"I was the representative of the church, of the state, of society."

"Then you must have been officious."

"Being officious is a role I play at weddings. It is not my nature. I am officious for hire."

"Could a coyote come to a wedding?"

"Absolutely *not*! The last thing we want at a wedding is a trickster. Though usually the best man tries to play the role. He likes to fumble in his pockets as though he had lost the ring. I smile, and in a low growl say, "Give me the ring or I will *knee* you! That shocks him into behaving."

"I'm impressed you'd be so direct. I thought weddings were pious affairs."

"Oh, they are! I make sure of that! I tell the bride and groom that after we are clear on what they want to have happen, I will see that that is what happens. They just have to do what I say. No ad-libbing. I am very heavily into control at weddings. That is what I am paid to do."

Coyote grinned. "That seems a little out of your laissez-faire character."

"Right! I ask the bride if there's anyone likely to cause trouble. 'Like who?' she says. 'Like your mother,' I say. She grins. 'Oh-h-h-h, my *mother*!' Often in Santa Fe there is no mother at the wedding; that is why they eloped to Santa Fe. Sometimes the mother is scheduled to fly in the morning of the wedding when it's too late to change anything. But sometimes we have to deal with the mother at the wedding, so I tell the bride I outrank even her mother."

"You *do* live dangerously."

"I enter into a conspiracy with the bride. I say tell me what you want to do, and then I will tell your mother that is the way our liturgy *always* goes; there are absolutely no changes permitted in the liturgy. The bride loves it, and she is all smiles as she walks down the aisle on her father's arm."

"You are very devious. I am just a little shocked."

"It all started with a mother of the bride who was terrorizing the bride five minutes before the wedding. I assumed my best Old Testament prophet stance and said, 'Madam, you go sit down in the front row and don't let me hear another thing from you!' She stalked off thinking 'That awful man!' The bride cried on my robe for thirty seconds, and then we were down the aisle all smiles. Except her mother's lips were so tight they about fell off."

"She might have slugged you with her purse."

"Combat pay."

"So, hey, why do you humans get married? Why don't you just have a party and move in together? Do you perform some kind of magic in the wedding ritual?"

"I don't perform magic, Coyote. If the couple believes there's magic in the ceremony, then there is. If they believe they have a very special relationship, then they do. If they say before their friends and relatives that their relationship is very special, then it is. If they say it in a church or a sacred grove or a meadow with a robed person, then perhaps they believe it even more. I don't 'pronounce' them man and wife. I say 'you have made a marriage, and we here are glad to recognize it.' The state doesn't make a marriage. A marriage happens between two people, and the state simply recognizes that it exists."

"Do you have un-marrying ceremonies?"

"A few progressive people have tried it, but it seems too civilized to be bearable by two people who are most likely feeling uncivilized toward each other."

"But it makes sense."

"Coyote, if humans did what makes sense, there would be no need for clergy, lawyers, or politicians. Un-marrying could be, theoretically, as civilized as marrying, but it almost never is. I urge people who are un-marrying not to do any more damage than necessary to the remaining goodwill. Which often puts me in direct opposition to the attorneys, but I have a different agenda from the attorneys. I told one woman, 'You have twenty years and two children together. Keep as much as you can of the goodwill and respect for each other.' Later she said she and her husband had sat together at their son's graduation, sharing their pride in him. People have to be very strong and intentional to pull off a civilized un-marrying. The benefits of doing so are great for both of them and for their children, but very few people can rise above their anger at the time of un-marrying."

"Maybe if there was that much goodwill, they should have stayed married."

"People have their reasons for un-marrying. The process could be much less destructive, but our society encourages the most destructive behavior when people un-marry. Which may be what keeps unhealthy marriages together."

"You are a bit gloomy about the whole institution."

"Not at all. I am an enthusiast for marriage. I enjoy weddings. I just think people put very heavy trips on the whole institution. People take marriage too seriously. It's supposed to be fun!"

"You, sir, are a *nut*!"

"No, merely an optimist!"

"You've been a groom a few times. How did it feel from that side? Did your having officiated hundreds of times make it any cooler being a groom?"

"Absolutely not! Pure terror every time."

"So the bride and the groom are always in shock?"

"The groom is always in shock. He looks like he's been pole-axed. I always remind him to smile when the bride comes down the aisle, so she won't have to see this slack-jawed catatonic groom waiting for her. He can't believe he is in the front of the church and the music is for him!"

"And the bride?"

"The bride is radiant, but on the edge of hysteria. I always tell the bride, 'If there is one place you will get into hysterics, it is when the ring won't go on the groom's finger. *Do not panic!*' So the ring sticks and she is about to panic; then she looks at me and I smile a sublime smile of 'I told you so, see?' and she relaxes. Then I pray while she composes herself."

"So those are some of the practical reasons for the elements of the wedding service? The prayer is so the bride can compose herself?"

"Well, Coyote, it is *also* a sacred moment!"

We punched each other and laughed, and then when we had composed ourselves, I asked him:

"So how about you? You've been domesticated a few times yourself."

"The bachelor's life is no life for me," said the Trickster. "I don't understand why you humans have to get God and the State of New Mexico into what is really something intensely personal. What does God care about who you live with and love? For that matter, why should the State of New Mexico care?"

"The horrible truth, Coyote, is that a great deal of what the traditional wedding symbolizes is the idea of woman as property. The marriage ceremony is supposed to make her feel better about it. She comes down the aisle under the protection of her father and is turned over to the protection of the groom. The groomsmen are the groom's armed men who are there to make sure he got what he paid for in the bride-price. The bride's father pays for the wedding in order to show off his wealth."

Coyote asked thoughtfully, "I thought we were talking love."

"We are, of course. We are also talking property. We are talking the protection of minor children. The State of New Mexico is a party to the marriage contract. The contract can not be dissolved without the state's permission, the state wants to know how the minor children are going to be supported and cared for. Even though a lot of us think the state unfortunately doesn't do a very good job of supporting and caring for minor children nobody else is looking out for."

"Do you tell this to the bride and groom?"

"Of course. It is usually a shock. They thought they were just in love and that's all there was to it. They didn't expect the the whole State of New Mexico was going to get in bed with them."

"I can see why you are officious. This marrying is very heavy."

"It's heavier than that, Coyote. I say it is something mystical that comes out of the history of the human race. Maybe even deeper; out of the whole story of sexual attraction and the forming of completeness, the forming of new life, out of two disparate contrasting beings. People say it's for better or worse, not just for the weekend. That goal makes it magical and mysterious. Sometimes I tell the bride and groom in the service that all of us admire their courage in getting married, especially those of us who *are* married. Lot of suppressed laughter in the congregation. 'Man's talking about *you*, dear!' Yes, there is mystery and magic about human weddings. That is why people are so terrified and hysterical and happy and panicked all at the same time."

"I like our way better," said Coyote.

"What's your way?"

"Well, it involves a lot of sniffing . . . It seems to work. You never see coyotes in divorce court. We don't need the State of New Mexico to tell us what our obligations are to our offspring. And we don't have much use for property or patriarchal symbols."

We were at the Loretto Chapel. I parked in the lot and got my robe out of the back seat.

"You're right, Coyote, maybe we've made something that ought to be simple too complex. And without love, there isn't much point in marriage, despite property and custom and patriarchy."

We gave each other a hug.

"Want to come in and watch a wedding in the chapel? I can sneak you in."

"No," he said, "You've made it sound too heavy for me."

I went in and calmed the bride and got the groom in the right place. The wedding march was fine and bride didn't trip on her gown ascending the steps to the altar. I was breathing easy until I put my hand out to the best man for the ring. He fumbled through all his pockets.

"Give it to me!" I hissed, and looked him threateningly in the eye.

I saw a yellow eye and a furry nose and a wide toothy grin and two paws protecting his groin.

It took the groom's parents and bride's parents together to get me calmed down enough to continue the service. I nearly got the giggles again during the benediction. After the service I apologized to the groom for my total loss of control and gave him back the fee. He said to keep it. This was his fourth marriage and much the most memorable. Eventually we found the best man bound and gagged in the balcony. I tried to explain it to him, but he said he'd rather have a glass of champagne and forget the whole thing.

COYOTE WANTS TO KNOW WHY JESUS WAS CRUCIFIED

isiting in Houston, I went to the auto show at the Astrohall. I got in the front of a Range Rover and was aware of someone lolling in the back seat, wearing a fur coat. I swung around, and there was a wide toothy grin.

"What are you doing in Houston?" I asked.

"We are everywhere, bubba!"

"Why are you at a car show?"

"Bright lights, pretty ladies, suckers lapping it all up. My kind of place. Can I cut you a good deal on this well-upholstered cactus crusher?"

"No way! I am only sitting here because if I sat in one in Santa Fe, the owner would call the police. Only fat wallets can sit here."

"Aw, too bad, baby," he said in mock sympathy. Then his eyes narrowed. "You don't perchance have any thoughts about trading in the VW do you?"

I felt guilty, and besides he was interfering with my private fantasies. I said, "Wouldn't you like me to drive you through the desert in air-conditioned elegance with the stereo playing? Impress the jack-rabbits?"

"Can't you see us in our Banana Republic outfits with a wine cooler in the tonneau? The jack-rabbits would be hysterical! We are too far gone to impress anyone, even jack-rabbits."

"Coyote, you are taking away my fantasy! You shouldn't take away my fantasy." I pouted and hit him.

He pulled me out and dragged me toward Joe Isuzu's pick-up truck display.

"You are a nice guy, Reverend. Let me show you something in a stripped plain brown pick-up."

"Nice guys finish last," I sighed.

He stopped and looked thoughtful.

"You're right! Why is that? Why do nice guys finish last?" He grinned. "Glad I'm a coyote."

"So," I said, "You must be a nice guy. You always finish last."

"Me? Me, finish last? Why do you say I finish last?"

"I've seen those Roadrunner cartoons. You never catch the roadrunner. The trick is always on you, even though it's your own trick."

He opened the door of a Cadillac, and we got in.

"You're right. I wonder why guys as nice as us always finish last. It doesn't make sense."

"Of course it makes sense. It's the American way. If you don't want to finish last, be a Donald Trump. That's the way the world is, Coyote."

"No, it's not. What was it Jesus said? He wouldn't have said it if it wasn't true."

"You mean about the meek inheriting the earth?"

"That's it! That's another way of saying nice guys, and nice gals, too, of course, eventually overcome the drawbacks of being nice and inherit the earth. See, here we are sitting in this nice Cadillac."

"It's not our Cadillac, Coyote, and I have a feeling we're not going to inherit it."

We sat there in silence while the Cadillac entertained us with its instrument panel.

"Tell me," said Coyote, "Was Jesus wrong?"

"Wrong about the meek inheriting the earth?"

"Yeah," he said. "I mean, he was killed even though he was quite a guy, right? He was on the side of the little people, on the side of the peace-makers and the meek and the nice guys. He was on the side of all the people you'd prefer to spend time with, assuming you don't have a need to dominate others and impress yourself. Which you and I do not have, or we would be driving this Cadillac. Was Jesus wrong? He stuck up for the little people and the internal security people took him out! Talk about the injustice of capital punishment! He didn't kill anyone or rape anyone or hold up any banks or grocery stores. They executed him just the same, for God's sake."

"Some think that's why he was executed; for God's sake."

"How can one human execute another human for God's sake? That's nutty!"

"People do it all the time. Religious people. Let's get out of this Cadillac if we're going to talk religion. It seems inappropriate."

We moved to a nearby Jeep. While Coyote was figuring a way to steal the stereo, I tried to explain why Jesus was crucified.

"It's complicated, Coyote. As you know, not everyone agrees with us that humans are a little bit of good, a little bit of evil, and a lot of muddle in the middle."

"How else *can* you characterize humans?" he asked as he reached under the dash to trace the wiring.

"Some humans think they and their group are perfectly good and the rest are perfectly evil."

"That is absurb!"

Coyote yipped and shook his paw. "Found the hot wire."

"In Jesus' day there were people who really deeply believed that they should be pure. They believed one should uphold the law in everything. Such as, 'Thou shalt not steal,' Coyote."

"Hush, I've got it loose."

"These people lived out in the desert," I went on, "in a place called Qumran. They believed that everything in the city, in Jerusalem was so wicked that God was going to destroy it. They were out in the desert preparing a highway for their god. They thought all the evil kings and evil lawyers and evil tax-collectors and evil ordinary people were going to be wiped out. Especially the people who steal stereos!"

A yellow eye appeared from under the dash. "Save the sermonizing for church, will you?"

I went on. "The evil kings and the evil lawyers and the evil tax-collectors were perfectly happy to have the pure in heart living out in the desert where they would not upset anyone in the city. They were not bothered by the threat of God's wrath anymore than such people are today. It was very frustrating to the pure in heart in those days, as it is in our time, to see the evil prosper. The pure in heart were torn between hoping the evil would mend their ways and be saved and hoping they *wouldn't* and would get what they deserved."

A muffled voice from under the dash said, "Those pure in heart sound real mean."

"Only the pure in heart can afford to be mean. The rest of us need to be forgiven in the same measure as we forgive. The pure in heart do not know what the rest of us know, which is the need for all humans to forgive all other humans."

Coyote appeared in the driver's seat. He was resentful. "You know what? This is a phony stereo! Why would anyone put a phony stereo in a car?"

"Maybe they're a sinner, too, and knew you were coming."

He laughed and relaxed and hung a leg out the door.

"You're right," he said. "It does give me a sense of comradeship with the human race to know they knew we were coming with larceny in our hearts. I couldn't relate to anyone who was pure in heart."

He hugged me and licked my face.

I pushed him away.

"Speak for yourself," I said. "I *buy* my stereos."

"But you got a nice job. I am a lily of the field. I got that line from Jesus, right out of the Gospels."

"So maybe you can finish the story of Good Friday."

"Sure. Jesus was among the pure in heart. He got to be that way through his cousin, John the Baptist, who got to be that way from the people out at Qumran, the people of the Dead Sea scrolls. As long as the pure in heart stayed out of town, the people in the city, whom they thought were evil, ignored them. But John the Baptist and Jesus came into town with their message attacking the kings and priests and lawyers and tax collectors. They said things were coming to an end very soon, and when the end came *bad* things were going to happen to the top dogs."

"And the crowd liked that?"

"The crowd always loves that. Deep down in every crowd is an envy of the upper-class. It's like the pure in heart being so mean. All the ordinary people in the crowd are just trying to get by, be nice guys, feed the kids, keep a dry roof over their heads. They would love to see the upper class get theirs, suffer a little, you know? Jesus announces he is the main man of the pure in heart and he is going to confront the evil priests. There's going to be a hot time in Jerusalem. Revolution and fiesta all in one."

"And the big guys? How do they feel?"

"How do the big guys feel? Like they always feel. They don't like it at all. The big guys don't want pickets at the White House or in Red Square.

The big guys don't want change. If there's going to be a change, the big guys won't be big guys anymore."

"So they arrested Jesus and crucified him?" I asked.

"You got any other theory?"

"There *is* another theory!"

Coyote looked surprised.

"The other theory is that there is this battle going on in the soul of every human between light and dark, between being decent and being a cynical rip-off artist. There is a struggle in every human between being good and being bad."

"With most of them most of the time in the middle in a muddle."

"Yes, the human condition is mostly in the middle in a muddle. But still there's this polarity."

"What's that got to do with Jesus?" asked Coyote.

"The theory is that Jesus was God as well as human; that in Jesus God came down into a human life, took on human form, and went around saying the things that God might say. Which is that you people should stop being larcenous and start caring for the widow and the orphan and the person who is forced to make a living soliciting in the streets. What God found out through that experience was that people didn't want to hear what God had to say. Just as people these days don't want to hear what the environmentalists have to say. What God found out in the incarnation is that people were so unwilling to hear what God was saying in the person of Jesus that they silenced him."

"And what did God do then?"

"The story is that God spent three days in the tomb thinking things over. On Easter Sunday, God rolled away the door of the tomb and announced a change of plans for humans. No longer would salvation be a matter of following the rules to the letter. No one can follow the rules all the time. Besides, life is no fun if it's all following the rules. Further, it was the king and the priests and the tax-collectors and the lawyers who made up the rules, not God. So, announced God on Easter, the way to being made whole, the way to salvation henceforth was not to be by following the rules but by having in your heart the best image you could imagine of being human and then try to be that. For Christians, that is the image of Jesus. But it might be a different image for others. Whatever, have in your mind the best image of being human and then do your best to be that. That way you will become a whole human being, a holy human being."

"That's what God said, huh?" interjected Coyote.

"That's what God said in *my* story!"

"What did God do after God came out of the tomb and made this announcement?"

"God disappeared. Some say God hasn't been seen on earth since. Some say God left a holy spirit to help us be human. Some say God enjoyed being human so much that God keeps on incarnating in humans, and sometimes you can see the holy glow in human faces. In a smile or a caring word."

"And that's it?"

"There's more to it. According to the story it is not important that nice guys, and nice gals, finish last. What gets you ahead on earth is not necessarily what gets you ahead in the spiritual world."

"Where does that happen?"

"Some say in a resurrection after this life."

"I don't think you believe *that*," scoffed Coyote. "What's *your* payoff?"

"It's hard to put into words, Coyote. I can *feel* it better than I can say it. Jesus said when you lose your life, you find it. It's the idea that if you go with the loser-winner model of life, eventually and inevitably you lose. You lose it *all*. So it is important to move to a different spiritual model; that spiritual maturity is becoming the finest human being one can become. If a person can do that, then life is much less of a rat-race with you being one of the rats. Instead we see a spiritual life in which all our life experience, good bad, the muddle in the middle . . . *all* our life experience become instruments of our deeper spiritual and emotional understanding. We become more aware, more alive, fuller in our love of other humans. Even in our love of furry thieving Tricksters. We no longer pretend to be pure in heart. We are simply alive. A little good, a little bad, and a muddle in the middle."

"That's your picture of spiritual fulfillment?"

"I think that's as good as it can get."

"You have convinced me that there are spiritual dividends in being a nice guy."

He took the gearshift knob out of his pocket and screwed it back on the gearshift of the Jeep.

He put his paw on my shoulder, and as we walked to the exit, he said;
"Those rich folks in their Range Rovers are really jealous of us having enough strength of character to enjoy a funky old yellow VW, right?"
"Right!" I said, "They don't make 'em like that anymore!"
We laughed our way right out of the Astrohall.

COYOTE LOOKS AT DEATH AND WONDERS WHAT IT IS

avajo stories about Coyote tell that he convinced the people that death is necessary. If there were no death, the world would become too crowded to live.

So I asked him, "Coyote, how come you excepted yourself from death?"

He looked surprised. "I die all the time. Haven't you read the other stories of me?"

"Yes, you die. But you have the ability to bring yourself back to life, so it really doesn't count."

He was defensive. "Jesus did it once."

"True, but he promised to take everyone with him off to a better place."

"So, be a Christian!" he said, huffily.

"You know I'm not a Christian, I tried, but I couldn't do it."

"Well, if you're going to ask difficult questions, I wish you'd just stop believing in me, too!"

"Come on, Coyote, you know you're part of me. I have to believe in you even when I'd rather not. We're in this together, minor deity and minor minister. People want to know what death is about?"

"Why don't you try another line of work?" He was still annoyed.

"I've thought about it many times. But they're nice people. I like them. Somebody's got to think about these things for them since they find thinking about death depressing. They enjoy life very much, and they are not at all eager to give it up. Especially after they have discovered that the whole point of living is to do well enough to move to Santa Fe and ski and go to concerts and feel slightly superior to all the people who don't live in Santa Fe."

"Really? Are they like that? They *are* my kind of people!"

"Of course! So help me think about death."

We went down to the donut shop, and on the way I told Coyote about Job. Job had been living on a nice retirement plan in Santa Fe and consequently praised God regularly for the goodness of life. But the Devil made a wager with God that Job only loved God because God was so good to him. Perhaps confident, perhaps insecure, God was stung by the Devil into a wager. The Devil took away all that Job had, betting that Job would curse God when the blessings disappeared. So Job was broke and sick and all his friends looked askance at him because, as all good Americans know, the poor and the sick have brought it on themselves and shouldn't expect the rest of us to take care of them.

"So, what's your point?"

"Well, Job thought it was terribly unfair. He hadn't done anything to deserve such treatment."

Coyote was puzzled. "What's unfair about it?"

"Job was *righteous*, but he was being *punished*! The *un* righteous *weren't* being punished! They were living in a half-million dollar house and driving a Mercedes."

"Life's like that. What did you expect?"

"It's unfair! Why should good innocent people suffer?"

"You *are* confused! You never should have gone to that Christian seminary. There is *no connection* between being good and being fortunate. Being good is its own reward. If people are good only so they won't suffer, that's kindergarten ethics. You're suggesting that millions of Jews and Christians and even some atheists operate on the kindergarten ethic that there is some connection between being good and having lots of toys."

"That's true."

Coyote then proceeded to explain the story of Job to me.

"Job is a story of spiritual progression. Job progressed from a kindergarten ethic to a justice ethic. He became outraged at inustice on the part of God. That's good. People *should* be outraged at injustice. The trouble is they are outraged at the wrong source of injustice. They should be outraged at *human* injustice. Injustice is a human problem, and if humans would just grow up, they might learn that a society based in justice and compassion is a better place for everyone to live. But that doesn't have anything to do with God!"

"So what about things that just *happen*?" I protested. "I have to do funerals for children. Why should they die? One happy little boy had a stroke. Another died of complications from a routine operation. They were young and innocent and had a whole life before them. They never had a chance to go through this spiritual transformation you talk about."

"You're right," said Coyote. "There is such a thing as real tragedy.

"And what is the meaning of real tragedy?"

"Hey, I am only a minor deity. I don't have the answer to that, if there is an answer to that. Maybe not everything has an answer. Maybe if I'd designed the Universe, I'd have corrected that fault but I'd have made others. Pain and tragedy just seem to be part of the experience of being alive."

He looked sad and ate my donut. Then he went on.

"What Job finally realized was the wild crazy magic of the Universe. The Universe was not created to make humans comfortable. That was Job's basic misperception, and all humans have it. It is known as the fallacy of central position. Relativity tells us that every point may function as a center around which everything else revolves. Humans see themselves as the center for which the Universe exists. Artistically, that's kitsch. Spiritually, that's kitsch, too. However, because Job was honest about his complaint against God's perceived injustice, God permitted Job to see into the whirlwind and understand the whole mystic picture. Which is that God is both creator and destroyer, dancing a wondrous dance of energy. That is much more magnificent than Job's kindergarten ethic or his lawyer's ethic. Job simply had to shut his mouth in awe! Which is where I was coming from when long ago I suggested to the early humans that they accept death as part of the dance of energy to make room for future humans."

I sipped my coffee and meditated. Then I said,

"But death is so *personal*, Coyote! *You* don't understand that, Coyote! It's one thing to see the big picture and be philosophical about death; but it *always* gets down to personal cases, Coyote! *That's* what tears people up. Facing their own dying. Losing their lovers. Losing friends. *That's* what tears people up, Coyote!"

"I know. You think I don't, but I do. The gods have the same problem. Old Pan died when Jesus came into his own. Pan just disappeared from lack of worship. It's the same with Coyotes. We're an endangered mythical specie."

"*NO!* Coyote, you *don't* understand! Mythical semi-divine figures cannot understand the personal existential horror of having to face one's personal existential non-being. That is pure terror, Coyote! *Only* humans understand it! Animals don't understand it and mythical semi-divinities don't understand it, either!"

As if by magic, just then a member of the church came by, plunked down a book, said, "Hi, boys!" and left.

"What a handsome lady Coyote," said Coyote.

"Come by church, and I'll introduce you."

We looked at the book. It was *The Paradox of Intention*, subtitled "Reaching The Goal By Giving Up The Attempt To Reach It." It was by Marvin Shaw*. Turned out Coyote knew what was in it, and after he explained it, I knew I had known it, too. It was typical Trickster art.

"The paradox of intention," said Coyote, "is that you can't get to spiritual fulfillment by *willing* to get to spiritual fulfillment. That is a basic truth of many religious systems. The paradox of intention happens for humans personally and individually. If we can understand the paradox of intention, we can understand the fear of dying. Perhaps then you humans of today can come to terms with your dying, even as the early people did.

"Look," he continued, "You're right about humans being the only ones who have to face in advance the existential terror of their personal death. Animals don't know about that, and the gods just go on doing what they do until no one believes in them anymore and they disappear. So humans know something special. Humans know, even if they won't admit it, that death is part of life, with no exceptions for good behavior. I grant you that. What humans need to understand is what that really means. When humans understand what that really means, humans can have an ecstasy of spirit which animals and gods do not experience."

"You have caught my interest."

I ordered more coffee and donuts and settled in for some spiritual enlightenment.

"Marvin Shaw contrasts the religion of acquisition with the religion of consolation. Job was into the religion of acquisition. He had lots of good stuff. His children were beautiful and had married well. He had status and honor. He was insecure because he had so much! American culture is a secular version of Job; we work hard to acquire; acquire stuff, acquire

*Shaw, Marvin C. *The Paradox of Intention: Reaching the Goal By Giving Up The Attempt To Reach It*, 1988, Scholars Press.

learning, acquire reputation. Calamity can wipe it out. Death will certainly wipe it out. A universal human predicament from the Stoics to the
Christians to the contemporary Americans; from Buddhists to the pre-
Christian semitics. Whether atheists or god-fearers, the good life is de-
fined by human common sense as the acquisition of things, power, love.
The more we have, the more terror we have at losing it all. If we believe
in the religion of acquisition, to lose our acquisitions is to lose our reason
for being. Which is why in America, you would think no one is ever
going to die. To die is the ultimate *faux pas*.

"The religion of consolation counsels a reversal. You reach the goal by
giving up the effort to reach it. The choice is whether we see life as hold-
ing on tight, or whether we see life as a flow, as becoming and leaving
and becoming again in another way all through life, and maybe even
afterward. The religion of consolation offers humans solace for having
to die. But solace cannot be acquired through effort, for if you acquired
solace through effort, you would fear losing it, and it wouldn't *be* solace.
It would simply be one more anxiety.

"In all the religions that Shaw looks at, including one school of psycho-
therapy, consolation is a free gift that comes when one has given up the
search. That is what happened for Job. That is what happened in Pauline
Christianity. It is true, for Stoics and Buddhists and Taoists. It was true
for Walt Whitman, as American a poet as ever sang. He discovered in
Song of Myself a mystic union with all life, even with all non-life.

"Victor Frankl, a therapist Shaw has studied, states that happiness can
never be caught by pursuing it, the U.S. Declaration of Independence
not withstanding. Happiness can come only as a side benefit from doing
something else. He says happiness comes as a side benefit of doing something that has meaning. Most of the great classic meanings are now
suspect, so it probably is a matter of personal meaning. Acting in a loving
fashion often has the side effect of making you happy. Working for a
cause you believe in often has the side effect of making you happy. One
doesn't love in order to be happy; one doesn't work for a cause to be
happy. You love because you love. You work for a cause you believe in.
Then you are surprised to find that, inadvertently it seems, you have
become happy. Being happy seems to be a free gift which comes from
the gods when humans are doing what humans are meant to do; which
is to *be* human: discover, do justice, love, dream.

"So it is with death. One does not go at death head-on. By the paradox of intention, you look at what *life* is. What life *really* is; deeper than acquisition. By looking at what life is, deeper than acquisition, you are surprised to find that death has lost its terror. It may not be scheduled as you personally would choose. Remember that brush you had with near-death? Your thought was, 'But I hadn't scheduled this!'

"Look at your being alive! Isn't it amazing you are here? You never asked to be here. You got life, and it's a mystery. You never think about how you got here. A little accident, and you might not have been conceived. Or maybe it was an accident you were conceived. Maybe if the iceman hadn't showed up that morning, you would have missed life altogether. You really don't know what it is to be conceived, and you really don't know what it is to be de-conceived. You might have missed the whole happening. Even worse than having totally missed it would be to be here and keep your eyes closed through the whole thing out of anxiety about the end of it. Having got what you never asked for, life, you might so fear losing it that you never got the joy and fun and wonder and delight of it.

"So many humans I see are doing just that. They waste their whole life wishing they were living some other life. They wish they were younger or a TV star or had a better love life or could get a new set of parents. Totally human, totally understandable. Oldest story in the world. Then suddenly, 'OK, time's up!' "

Coyote was really hot. The counter-girl was fascinated, kept hovering around filling our cups. Some of Coyote's eloquence was for her benefit, but I was moved by it, too.

"Wouldn't you rather embrace life than hide from it? Our awareness of our dying shows us what the religion of acquisition does; makes us hide where God won't see us and make a bet with the Devil about our spiritual condition. Better to understand that *your* life is set in the context of Life which is set in the context of a Universe which has the qualities of space and time. In that Universe all things are changing, whirling, boiling, creating, destroying. Stability is an illusion. Stability is a lie. In the whirlwind when God finally appeared, Job found Shiva, Creator and Destroyer. Creator and Destroyer; the two are always linked! They are the same. They are change. We are formed, even us gods, by little whirlpools of energy created by the entropy, the decline and dying, of the

Universe. We are born out of dying; when we die we give birth.

"So!" said Coyote, giving a wicked smile and a flourish of his tail, "Death is not just a damn annoyance to you humans. Death is something special which you realize and which is a yardstick about how well you're living. Death is a little prod in the back of your awareness which asks you if you're hiding from life. Death is a little voice that wonders why you are spending this life wishing you were in a fantasy life.

"I have to admit," he said, "death is not so hot. It *is* scary. But as I told the first humans, it is necessary to make the whole thing work. If you really accept the gift of life, which most humans don't, then you have no problem with death. By the paradox of intention, when you try to avoid death, you only avoid life. Paradoxically again, when you really accept your own death, life becomes tasty and tangible and sensual. Then death is only a transformation back to whatever was before life."

The counter-girl came up with the tab. Coyote grinned and disappeared. I suppose she thought I had been talking to myself. People often do that in the donut shop.

I came out into a gloomy winter day with snowflakes in the air. I thought to myself what a lovely day! How beautiful the snowflakes are! I had a flat tire. A really nice kid from the service station fixed it, and I thought how fortunate I was there were such good people in the world! As I rattled off I thought how glad I was that my father had seduced my mother or the other way, whichever on that August evening long ago, the result of which was what I egocentrically define as the major event in my personal story. I hoped my return to the great unknown would have some of the same quality of ecstasy as my conception did.

Coyote reappeared in the backseat.

"Hey, man, put the top down."

"You're crazy, Coyote, it's snowing!"

"Yeah! I love to ride with the top down when it's snowing!"

"But *you* don't die when you catch pneumonia!"

"Oh, yeah. I forgot!"

And he disappeared.

I stopped and put the top down, and as happens with New Mexico weather, immediately the sun came out.

Coyote and Doña Coyote Ride Up Elk Mountain And We Explain Things To Each Other

leven-fifty a.m. September 26

I leave Santa Fe on St. Francis Drive.

12:00 noon

As arranged, I pick up Coyote and Doña Coyote on the east bound ramp to Interstate 25.

Doña Coyote was pleasant and friendly. Coyote looked rather subdued. His face was brushed and his paws were clean. I had a sinking feeling that things were not going to go well.

Doña Coyote said, "It was certainly nice of you to offer us this trip up Elk Mountain. We haven't been back to the Pecos since we moved into Santa Fe."

Coyote smirked and said, "He gets big money from church members for this trip. He's doing it for us because he likes us."

There was a little silence and Doña Coyote said, ". . . and because he needs a sermon."

Coyote started to say something and then bit his tongue. He stared out the window.

They were sitting in back, but I could see them in my wide-view rear-view mirror.

"Hey," I said, "Relax! We're out for fun, and if I get a sermon for the folks when I get back, why that's a side issue. Come on, let's enjoy ourselves!"

There was a moment of silence. Then Doña Coyote said, "Well, why didn't Nancy come?"

I had to fake it. "Oh, she has allergies," I said.

"To coyotes?" asked Doña Coyote with a certain tone in her voice.

"No! No! to chamisas and grasses and stuff. Oh, she *loves* coyotes!"

"Well, I just wondered," said Doña Coyote.

Another period of silence.

12:15 p.m. Coyote observes that I have new side curtains. "Nice," he says.

"Right, nice," I say.

So we go along in silence for awhile, and I think well I will just drive them up the mountain and drive them down the mountain and then go to my office and make up some story. I start thinking about how it could have been with us happily discussing important things. I hear nothing from the back seat, and then I look in the rear view mirror, and they are smooching back there. Coyote opens one eye, winks, and then closes it again.

12:22 A very large bug smashes itself directly in front of my eyes. With a whole windshield to choose from, why does the first bug after leaving the gas station always smash into the little spot of windshield just in front of the driver's eyes? Do not tell me the universe is neutral. The universe gets its kicks out of being troublesome, difficult, petty, mean.

Coyote said, "Oh, stop it. The universe is not mean and petty and out to get you. The universe is magnificently unaware of you."

"You'd think differently if you had a windshield," I responded.

We came into Pecos and stopped for lunch. Doña Coyote and Coyote seemed perfectly at ease, and the waitress greeted them warmly and cheerfully. I felt uneasy still, but we filled up on something covered with green chili and lots of strong coffee. I was very conscious of my midsection, but we put the top down and roared off into a lovely cool fall day to conquer Elk Mountain.

Doña Coyote belched happily and grinned and said, "Thanks for the great lunch. I'm sorry I was so rude before."

"No problem!" I said, and we all grinned at each other and went careening up the road to Terrero.

1:20 p.m. We came up behind a pickup composed of panels painted three different colors travelling 25 in a 40-mile an hour zone, complete with no passing lines in the road.

"Pass him!" said Coyote.

"Too dangerous," I said.

"Honk at him! Make him get out of the way!"

"Just make him go slower," observed Doña.

Coyote was irate! "What's the idea of going 25 in a 40-mile an hour zone? Who does he think he is going under the speed limit? He ought to be arrested."

"Maybe he's enjoying the beautiful day," I said.

"He could enjoy it just as much going over the speed limit as under the speed limit," said Coyote. He sulked.

We came to a passing zone. I passed. Coyote started to make some sort of sign to the driver, but Doña Coyote grabbed his arm and put a hammer-lock on him. He glared at her, and then they both laughed.

"So," said Coyote, "You wanted to explain things, or have things explained to you. What needs explaining?"

It was such a lovely day I couldn't think of anything that needed explaining except maybe why it couldn't always be such a lovely day.

Doña Coyote said, "You're right; nothing needs explaining on a day like this. It's only when things are going badly and we're unhappy that things need explaining. Which really means only you humans have to ask for explanations because the rest of us animals are pretty happy most of the time."

"How come you're happy most of the time?" I asked.

"Because we don't ask for explanations," she said. "You humans keep asking for explanations, and then when you never get any that satisfy you, you want an explanation for that. And when you don't get an explanation for not getting an explanation, you get angry and depressed."

"Definitely sounds like some people I know!"

Coyote said, "The only thing I think needs explaining is why people don't have a good time. To me the purpose of being alive is to enjoy being alive. Eating well, playing a few little tricks here and there, keeping them laughing. If you concentrate on the good times, you don't need any explanations!"

Doña Coyote said, "Come on, Coyote! It's a little deeper than that. It's more than a good time. It has to do with works of love. It means your family and your friends and being decent to the other creatures. It means loving responsibility, not just hedonism."

He beamed at her. "Of course, my sweet! How could I forget that? Thank you for reminding me." And he kissed her enthusiastically.

She smiled demurely and kissed him back.

I thought to myself I didn't need to drive up Elk Mountain for *that* insight! I wanted to bring back something deep; a theological trophy for the pulpit. I was getting bromides; obvious truths!

"'Kitsch' is the word you're looking for," said Doña Coyote.

I began to wonder why I invited her!

1:35 p.m. We come to a major rock slide; a cliff-slide.

"Pretty impressive," I said. "Shows the power of nature! Makes you feel insignificant!"

Coyote said, "Maybe it makes *you* feel insignificant. It doesn't make *me* feel insignificant."

"What if it landed on you?"

"I would be dead. But that doesn't have anything to do with whether I feel insignificant. A rock-slide is a rock-slide. I am a Coyote. Why would a Coyote feel insignificant when confronted by a rock-slide?"

"It has to do with feelings of power," said Doña Coyote. "Humans like the reverend here are concerned with power. Most of the time they ignore the power of nature, so when they see the power of nature they are surprised. They feel powerless compared to a rock-slide. They feel insignificant if they don't feel their personal power."

"You're right, my dear," said Coyote. "You have just explained why humans tend to avoid nature and try to control nature. You have just explained why humans don't get excited by the wildness of nature. They have performance anxieties. They cannot move continents. They cannot change the stars in their courses or the seasons. They cannot accept that all living things are puny and finite. So they don't want anything to do with it. They prefer an artificial environment made to their own specifications."

I thought to myself, "Damn rock-slide!" I popped the clutch and we proceeded up the mountain. The colors were magnificent: yellow, green, blue, white, orange-grey cliffs. The air was cool and clear and sweet.

I said to my friends, "Maybe besides enjoying being alive and besides our loving duties, maybe there is a need for just appreciating the beauty of nature. Maybe we are here to love the universe and appreciate it and revel in it."

"So," Coyote said, "You think the purpose of humans is to be an audience for the divine show?"

Doña Coyote punched him in the ribs. "Coyote, don't be a homo-sapiens' rear end!" Then she blushed slightly, and muttered, "Pardon me! That's what we animals call another animal who's being stupid."

We crested the top of the road, and there were the Sangre de Cristos spread out in a lovely blue haze. "Just look how grand they are!" I said.

Doña Coyote said, "What's that mean? Grand? That's a human judgement. That is irrelevant. The mountains *are*, that's all!"

We had stopped. I turned around and looked at them both directly. "Okay, so what's it all about? You tell me. I keep looking for the truth, but it all gets very ambiguous. I never seem to get a clear picture of what it's all about."

"That's good," said Doña Coyote. "When things get ambiguous, it means you may be getting near the truth. When it's really really clear, you can be sure it is not the truth, but someone fooling themself. The truth is ambiguous, so when things feel really ambiguous, the chances are you are getting close to the truth — which *is* ambiguous, which was *meant* to be ambiguous."

"You are telling me it's too big to understand?"

"Absolutely. Some of the scientists we have listened to in Los Alamos seem to recognize that, but most religious people cannot accept that. Most of your human religions would prefer to be clear, even though they are demonstrably wrong."

"Not all your religious efforts are wrong-headed," said Coyote. "Only your efforts to make clear what has to remain ambiguous."

"What are the valid religious efforts?" I asked.

"The private experience of ecstasy," he said. "We animals understand that."

"It's not always private, Coyote," said Doña Coyote. "We practice group religion when we gather to sing at the moon." She turned to me. "I hear some of our cousins sang to your group when you were camping near here at Jack's Creek."

"They sure did! Gave everyone the creeps."

"That's because God was there," she said.

"God was there?" I asked, amazed.

"Of course," she said. "When you humans gather in God's name and sing, you think God is there. When we animals gather in God's name and sing, God is there, too. Think you're the only ones on the planet who sing thanks to God? Having heard your congregation sing, I think there's more chance of God attending a coyote howl!"

I couldn't disagree.

I said, "I think the people I know are unsure about the direct experience of God, but they are certainly willing to experience the intricate wonder of that which is, commonly called the 'creation' which may imply a creator. Is that ambiguous enough?"

"Very good!" they said in chorus.

We decided after that we didn't need a peak experience, so we took a previously unexplored road which led down into a valley. It was an anxiety producer, and when I came to a stream, I stopped. "Gun it!" said Coyote. "I might get stuck," I said. Coyote gave me a look of disgust. I backed up to turn around.

2:10 p.m. Stuck in a seep cleverly disguised as grass growing on the edge of the road. I suggest they push while I get it rocking. Coyote looks disgusted. "We were not designed by the creator to push cars out of cow wallows," he says. "Not my karma," he says.

"And you're not my dogma," I say. "Push!"

"Let's go chase those cows," he says to Doña Coyote, and off he goes.

Doña Coyote said to me, "I'll keep you company."

So I got out the jack, jacked the rear wheel out of the mud, piled branches under it, let down the jack, and rocked it out of there. She exclaimed all the while how clever I was about it, and I found I actually enjoyed the whole experience. Coyote saw us drive off and ran after us. I would have let him run 'til he dropped, but Doña Coyote opened the door, and in he came, all furry and sweaty. I was muddy and sweaty, so we batted each other a few times and made up.

We felt greatly relieved at being unstuck and homeward bound.

"Did you hear about the lawyer who sued the dentist?" asked Coyote.

"No," I said.

"Claims the dentist pushed him into a root canal!" said Coyote.

"Do you think people are getting more cynical?" I asked. "All these lawyer jokes and the surveys on how people feel about political leaders and the debunking of everything by TV. Are people getting more cynical?"

"Yes," said Coyote, "People *are* getting more cynical, and that's good and healthy. Cynicism leads to belief!"

"That's novel," I said. "Everyone thinks cynicism leads to *dis*-belief."

"It does," he said.

"That's contradictory," I said. "You just said cynicism leads to belief, and then you agreed that cynicism leads to dis-belief."

"Right! Which is ambiguous. And we just got through saying that when we get close to ambiguity, we are getting closer to the truth."

"Please explain it to my lesser consciousness."

"Cynicism leads to disbelief in the accepted group beliefs of your culture. That is why the priests and politicians don't like cynicism in their followers. But cynicism leads people through the dis-belief in what the group thinks to a personal belief, a discovery and affirmation in later life of what you or I personally can believe in with all our heart and spirit."

"And what is that for you?" I asked him.

"Ultimately nothing matters but the days you remember when you had a hell of a good time."

I turned to Doña Coyote. "And what do you believe in?"

She said, "Ultimately nothing matters but the wonderful times you have with your friends."

They looked at me. "And you?" they said.

I blushed, but I had to say it, "Ultimately nothing matters but enjoying the gift of creation which is why we were created."

"Too grandiose," they said, "but utterly human. You are forgiven!"

3:05 p.m. We pull onto the highway and catch up with a pickup, this one blue and rust, doing 25 in a 40 mile zone.

"What is this?" asked Coyote. "A fad?"

"No," I said, "It's life in the slow lane, and there's only one lane."

"Oh," he said. "Well, it's lovely day for appreciating the scenery. Maybe you've got a point! Doña, enjoy the scenery! Act human!"

Now you know and I know what we humans all really want deep down is acceptance. I was overwhelmed with a deep feeling of acceptance by my two semi-divine friends.

Just then my hat blew off. I stopped alongside the Interstate, and since I couldn't backup, Coyote ran on back and got it for me. As I put it back on, Doña Coyote said, "That is the most dweebie hat! Where did you get that hat?"

"In Maine," I said.

"I thought so," she said, "Makes you look like George Bush."

We rode home in silence.

So much for acceptance by the gods!

COYOTE AND NEITZSCHE

I mentioned to Coyote that I wanted to do a sermon on Nietszche. I hoped he could help me with it. He gave me a level calm stare. It is an intimidating stare. I willed myself not to quail before it, but it had such power!

Coyote threw his head back, emptying his coffee cup. He put the cup down and wiped his lip with a furry foreleg. He said:

"I can't believe what I just heard. Why would I be interested in Nietzsche?"

"As a favor to me?" I asked.

"No," he said, "not as a favor to you."

"For the intellectual challenge?" I asked hopefully.

"I get all the intellectual challenge I need arguing with the other gods whether humanity was a good idea," he said.

"Whose side are you on?"

"I am for humans. I enjoy their garbage."

"Thanks," I said. "Now please come help me with a sermon on Nietzsche.

"I have to go to a funeral that day."

"What day?"

"Whatever day it was you had in mind."

"Whose funeral is it?" I asked.

"One of the gods. Died of malnourishment. You probably know him. The Marlboro Man."

I was shocked. "The Marlboro Man is dead?" I couldn't believe it.

"You heard it here first," he said.

A few days later I went to the donut shop and parked the car in back out of sight. I took an inconspicuous seat, hiding behind a newspaper and waited. I saw Coyote snoop around and look through the big window. Then he slipped in behind a large woman with several children, all of whom were exceedingly jolly.

I reached from behind my paper, grabbed Coyote's tail and held on hard. "Gotcha!" I said. He said something unprintable. I gave his tail a couple of half-hitches around the upright of the stool and said to him:

"Listen, bugger, you and I are going to discuss Nietzsche whether you want to or not!"

"Okay, Okay," he said, wincing. "Loosen up on the tail, will you? We're friends, remember?"

"Hope the funeral wasn't today," I said, "because you're staying here."

"Aw," he said with tears in his eyes, "Would I bug out on you, ol' buddy?"

"Not today you won't," I said. "At least not until I get a sermon for Sunday."

He sat down on the stool, which considerably lessened the tension on his tail, and said: "I do believe you have been reading some Nietzsche. The old will-to-power stuff, eh?"

I nodded. I said, "If you hadn't chosen to hang around civilization yourself for the easy sweets, you wouldn't be in this position of having a knot in your tail. You choose your own good. Badger and Eagle never come in here."

He cocked his head at me and dead-pan quoted Nietzsche. "Life neither possesses nor lacks intrinsic value, yet it always is being evaluated."

"Thank you, Frederick Coyote," I said. "Would you explicate this bit of doctrine?"

"What Brother Nietzsche meant," said Coyote, "is that evaluations of life are no reflection on life itself, which is neutral in terms of value. Life *is*! What value statements are are statements of the inner condition of the one doing the evaluting."

"An example, please."

"Consider that large lady with the large pleasant children sitting over there. Look at their faces, lips flecked with donut crumbs. They judge life to be glorious. Tomorrow the lady will try to get into her dress and will conclude that life is unfair and mean."

"You have become a moral relativist?" I asked.

"Brother Nietzsche invented the concept," he said. "Or at least he popularized the idea among the establishment philosophers of Europe in the early 20th century."

"And do you agree with the concept of moral relativism?" I asked.

He looked down his long nose. "The very idea! Me, a divine figure, be a moral relativist? What a shocking idea for you, a clergyman, to have!"

"In the stories about you among the native Americans, you act as though you have no morality at all."

"I have an absolute morality!" he said. "I am for me. And a few of my friends."

"What is the nature of this absolute morality?" I asked. "How does it work?"

He looked genuinely puzzled. He spread his paws to show he had nothing to hide. "It means I have the power to get what is good for me. The power to get what is good for me is good power. That which frustrates good power is bad. Is that simple enough for you?"

"There used to be another way," I said. "In the good old days there was the power of self-sacrifice."

"It seems a contradiction," he said sardonically. "How can sacrificing yourself be good? What could it get you?"

"Well," I said, "It did depend on a view of life. It depended on a view of life that says things are not what they seem. That things are in fact really just the opposite of what they seem. Those who lose their life will find it, and those who find their life will lose it. I believe that was Jesus' point of view."

"Yes!" he said. "And we know what happened to Jesus!"

"The Christians say he rose from the dead and sits at the right hand of God the Father and judges the nations of the earth."

"So you are saying the Christians claim you get power in the fullest sense by giving up power in this life?"

"That's what they say."

"But that's not what you say?"

"Most of the time, no," I said.

"You are unsure?" He was pressing the point.

I said, "I have reservations about the will-to-power being the definer of the good."

"You think there is some referent for the good other than the will-to-power of a person or a group of people?" He was circling for the kill.

He said, "You think there is some Transcendent Other by which the human judgements of good can be judged objectively?"

"It's conceivable," I said, lamely.

"Conceivable by whom?" He was salivating. His eyes were alight. There was silence. "Conceivable only by those who do not have power and therefore want to turn the world of the powerful upside down and make slaves the masters!" He licked his chops.

I played the innocent lamb. "You know," I said, "The German army put a copy of *Thus Spake Zarathustra* in the pack of every German soldier in World War I."

Coyote did a double-take and look suspiciously at me. "So?" he said.

"So," I said, "One of the uses of this moral relativity is that might makes right and marching young men off to death to further the power desires of the masters is good and honorable."

"The good tidings of the twentieth century!" he said.

"It required the death of God," I said. "Some philosophers thought the death of God was an improvement. Now at the end of the twentieth century we may have to reinvent the gods. And maybe goddesses."

He looked puzzled. "I thought you would like Nietzsche. He was influenced by Emerson, and you like Emerson."

"Emerson and Nietzsche lived in different times than ours," I said. "We may have to define the will-to-power as what is good for humanity. And even that may be exploitative of the other species." I went on. "Emerson and Nietzsche were trying to establish the glory of a new sort of human, a sort of super-human. Not in the sense that the Nazis used the term, but as the finest sort of noble humanist individual who embraced in self the contradictions of being human. That was a noble work of the nineteenth century minds. It inspired the imagination of the twentieth century. It was perverted into Naziism and Soviet collectivism. Now it has reached the limits of the will-to-power in the exploitation of the earth's finite resources. There is not enough wealth for us all to be people of wealth. Yet there is no longer any mythical outlet for the dreams of the slaves. Thus the dogs of class warfare and terrorism are loosed on the planet. Those in the life-boat are banging the third world with the oars. The third world threatens to bring down the whole human enterprise with nuclear weapons and poison gas and leave the oil fields in ruins."

I had a large gulp of coffee.

"So Nietzsche and Emerson are outmoded?" he asked.

"Outmoded as public policy," I said. "They are not outmoded as a valid basis for personal life."

"That seems contradictory," he said.

"It is contradictory," I said. "But that poses no terror for the super-person. The super-person understands that she or he as a human is composed of contradictions. The super-person affirms that contradiction as one of the contradictions to be held in dynamic tension within the self."

"Would you mind untying my tail?" he said. "It is beginning to lose sensation."

"You promise to stay to the end of the sermon?"

He gave me the Boy Scout salute, and I untied him. We ordered more donuts, and the world seemed better as the greasy little fellows gave their life that we might live and discuss the higher reasons for our being.

"What do you like about Nietzsche's Overman," he asked. "His super-person, as you say."

"There is much that is admirable and recommendable to people. Some of the characteristics of the super-person fit you, old semi-divine scavenger. And also some of the better, more interesting sorts of humans."

"Tell me," he said. He smiled broadly and licked a donut's sugar lasciviously.

I settled on the stool. "She, or he as the case may be, has organized the chaos of the passions. She or he knows and accepts and uses the passions. None of this denying the passions through intellect or spurious pious spirituality. Then the super-person creates a personal style. Nietzsche once said, 'Above all, do not mistake me for someone else!' Which might be a good spiritual question to ask ourself. Would anyone mistake you for someone else? Meditate on that koan."

"Then the super-person becomes creative," I went on. "Maybe not a giant of culture, but at least a person who is not merely a consumer of a pre-packaged culture. As you can see, the number of superpeople is a small minority compared to the herd. The super-person has organized his passions, given style to his character, and become creative. But that is not enough to qualify as a super-person. The super-person is fully aware of life's terrors and still affirms life without resentment. She becomes a philosopher. What religion is for the masses, philosophy is for the sage."

Coyote waved his paw expansively. "Wonderful!" he said. "Do you know any super-people? Can you name names?"

"Not the point, Coyote. The point is that for Nietzsche this is a sub-stitute for the god-figure. This is humanity moving beyond itself as far as humanity is beyond the apes. A few people may at times in their life be like the over-person, but it is not a state of perfection to be attained. It's a goal, Coyote. Nietzsche says a people's goals tell us a lot about them. What they value as good."

I thought a minute and then went on. "Nietzsche was prescient about one thing. He said the old morality was that if you are good, you will be happy. Nietzsche says that's not true. It is just the reverse. If you are happy, you will be good."

"I don't get it," he said.

"Example. Consider the ghettos of America," I said, "Our society says, 'Be good and you will be happy.' That suits the master-slave relation-ship. But it isn't true. Nietzsche knew what our government refuses to see, wills not to know. When evil exists, it is because the will-to-live has been frustrated. To say, 'Be good and you'll be happy' is a lie. Turn it around, and you understand that if people are happy, they will be good. If you wish to make the people in the ghetto good, you have to see that they are happy. To make them happy, you give them some power over their life. You do not exploit them! What a wonderful advisor Nietzsche would make to the White House."

"You dreamer!" he said.

"My problem as a clergyman," I said, "is that most religions are ded-icated to excusing the evil, making the slaves think there is a different spiritual world so they will live in this world in that illusion. I have been trying to convince people it is better to live without illusions. Those who live with illusions have to keep protecting their illusions. They cannot move to the virtures of the super- person; organizing their passions, living with style, and being creative."

"How do you resolve the power-over-others problem?" he asked.

"The super-person finds power in self-control, not control over others. The acme of power for the super-person is to be perfectly self-possessed; to have no fear of death or fear of any other person. The super-person has mastered the passions and lives a simple life. Which may be the necessary social policy link to living within the limits of the exploitation of the planet."

Coyote was silent. Then he asked slowly and quietly, "How does one know if one is getting close to super-personhood?"

"There is a simple but infuriating test Nietzsche proposes," I said. "He calls it the Doctrine of Eternal Recurrence. You ask yourself: Would I be willing to take my life just as it is without alteration on an eternally recurring basis? My limited survey shows that even people with good lives would want to make at least a few minor changes. Which means that they have not accepted life as it is. They are only willing to accept it as they would modify it if they had the power. Nietzsche says that if you would be willing to take it again just as it happened in every little detail, then you have accepted life. Then you are free of resentment. Then you are perfectly self-possessed. Then you live without fear of death or any person. You are then happy! And, if you are happy, you are then *good*!"

Coyote smiled, shrugged, and reached around and shook out his tail vigorously. "You know," he said, "Life's like a cartoon."

"Like a cartoon?" I asked.

"It's like those cartoons of the roadrunner and me. They get shown time and time again, and the same thing happens every time the cartoon gets shown. It doesn't ever change, no matter how many times you show the cartoon. The roadrunner always gets away. You know what? I wouldn't have it any other way. I just love that cartoon even though I know I am going to get blown to bits, flattened, made a fool of every time."

He smiled wistfully, slid off the stool, gave me a hug and a kiss. He went out into the night.

As he disappeared, trotting easily, I whispered to myself, "Now there's a god I can believe in!"

POSTSCRIPT
BY COYOTE

As I like to tell my friend the Minister, there are only two major problems for you humans. I don't mean things like wars or earthquakes or drought or taxes or lightning or just bad luck. Those are minor problems. Your first major problem is not listening. Most of the time most people are too busy with their own static to hear clearly what another person is saying. When you *are* listening but don't understand, you don't ask for clarification. So that's the first big problem for humans. And for me. At least half the stories the Navajo People tell of me have to do with me not listening because I was too smart. So the Trickster tricked himself (herself). The second big problem for humans is not telling the truth when speaking. Sometimes it's a lie up front. Often it's an attempt to protect. Sometimes it's a lie by the ego to the self. In the other half of the stories the People tell of my tricks, I am a liar in some way. The stories of the Trickster all have to do with either not listening to what's been said or not telling the truth. And almost always the trick backfires on the Trickster.

Well, don't laugh at *me*! *You*'re the people who make up these stories.

ALSO BY WEBSTER KITCHELL

Coyote Says . . . More Conversations with God's Dog

Coyote returns! In this triumphant sequel to *God's Dog,* the mischevious deity engages his minister friend in more playful banter about life, religion, and the universe. With humor and poignancy, they discuss luck, Easter, the Messiah, power, and more over coffee and during long drives through New Mexico.

Published by Skinner House Books

Available from the UUA Bookstore
25 Beacon Street
Boston, Massachusetts 02108
1-800-215-9076